Curtis Levang,

LOOKING GOOD OUTSIDE

FEELING BAD INSIDE

Emerald Books

P.O. Box 635 • Lynnwood, Washington 98046

ISBN: 1-883002-11-7

Published by
Emerald Books
P.O. Box 635
Lynnwood, WA 98046
tel. (800) 922-2143

Previously Published as THE ADAM AND EVE COMPLEX

Cover design by Chris Garborg
Illustrations by Eileen Crowley Habibi
Poems used with permission of Sarah Hall Maney
All scriptures quotes are from NIV unless otherwise noted.

Printed in the United States of America

Dedication

To my wife Lizz and my daughter Natalie.
You continually teach me how wonderful God's gifts are.

CONTENTS

FOREWORD

In 1983 I attended a workshop presented by a midwestern university professor who had emerged as an expert on the topic of shame. During the first session, as he defined shame and described the part it plays in a host of family problems, I sat spellbound. He was making sense of so many things that had been puzzling me. Every story, every illustration, every description struck a familiar chord. I felt overwhelmed as I realized the immense, destructive role shame played in the lives of most of the people I had counseled. Reeling with amazement at the immensity of the concept, I barely could sit still through the remaining hours of the workshop.

The following year, as I wrote *Good News for the Chemically Dependent*, the issue of shame almost engulfed the book. I had come to believe, and still do believe, that shame is the soil from which grow addictions and a host of other human problems. I also had come to believe that shame plays a continuing, destructive role in the lives of addicts and those who love them. My editor warned me to cut back the ballooning chapter on shame and keep the book focused on addiction. He advised that I save the shame theme for a future book, which became *Tired of Trying to Measure Up*.

Those experiences I had with shame, albeit as a counselor and author, seem to be universal. In my case, shame undermined my participation in a workshop and sidetracked the development of my first book. In the case of many people I have known, shame has undermined their participation in relationships and sidetracked their very lives.

Perhaps this explains my elation, even relief, at the publication of Dr. Curtis A. Levang's *Looking Good Outside, Feeling Bad Inside*. His book presents a fully integrated approach to psychology and theology, an excellent grasp of the phenomenon of shame; and empathy for those who struggle to be free from it. Most important, he places the discussion in an altogether biblical context. The result is a book with understanding and authority.

In my counseling practice I frequently need to refer a client to someone who uses a grace-full, steady, and understanding approach. I remember the satisfaction I felt after discovering that Dr. Levang was just such a helper. I can now refer people to his book as easily as I have been able to refer them to his counseling practice.

Dr. Levang asserts that shame is really a destructive message about who we are, the painful sense of being defective as a person. If this be true, then Christians have more to say about shame than anyone else. After all, we have a relationship with the Creator of the universe who has done something about who we are. With loving acts of redemption and re-creation, he has made us brand new creations. Because of Jesus, the good news is that we are acceptable to God. He declares to us, "There is now no condemnation."

—Jeff VanVonderen

PREFACE

As a son of an evangelical minister I was raised in a Christian environment. I cannot remember a time when I did not believe in Christ's forgiveness and the power of his word.

The people of my conservative background raised their collective eyebrows, however, when I began to pursue graduate studies in psychology. What could psychology teach that the Bible had not already revealed? To many sincere Christians, the two seem incompatible. After years of study and application I am convinced that the two not only are compatible, they are inseparable.

The blending of my Christian faith and the clinical expertise I have gained over the years has helped me bring spiritual and psychological healing to hundreds of clients. During my years of practice a popular concept, shame, has particularly interested me. As I have researched it—from both biblical and psychological viewpoints—I have applied it in my own life and the lives of my clients. The results have been very satisfying. It is this unique, Christian understanding of shame that I wish to share with you.

Coming to understand the power of the shame concept has motivated me to let other people know how strong its influence is. That is why I have written *Looking Good Outside, Feeling Bad Inside*. My confidence in this book's effectiveness is based on research and consultation with individuals and their families during almost fifteen years of clinical practice, a practice that has confronted the entire spectrum of psychological needs, from general problems to those of people in treatment centers and in prisons.

The people described in this book are real. I have worked with them. The issues in their lives may easily mirror yours or someone you care about. (Please note, however, that in order to maintain confidentiality I have carefully masked the identity of each person appearing in the book.) The solutions to the problems are just as real. I have seen their effects on the lives of my clients.

I believe that these solutions, the principles explained in *Looking Good Outside, Feeling Bad Inside,* can be just as effective in any of our lives. Although the principles may seem new, they are as old as the human race. I am convinced they are part of God's plan to restore us to wholeness.

My life is dedicated to helping people find that wholeness. There is nothing I would rather do.

—Curtis A. Levang
June 1992

ACKNOWLEDGMENTS

This book evolved over six years of research, dialogue, and inter-action with a great number of people, each of whom has helped shape my understanding of shame and grace. My thanks go to

. . . the staff of Passages Counseling Center, most notably Fred Peterson and Jeff VanVonderen, for giving me an opportunity to better learn about grace and live it.

. . . my colleagues, Dr. Joanne May, Carol Travilla, and Maureen McNeal, for encouraging me and continually believing in my work and ideas.

. . . my new friend, Charette Barta, for supporting me in prayer and sharing with me Isaiah 41:10 (RSV): "Fear not, for I am with you, be not dismayed, for I am your God; I will strengthen you, I will help you, I will uphold you with my victorious right hand."

. . . my editors, Nathan Unseth, for helping me over the rough transitions and bringing wisdom and direction to my writing; and for the unshakeable warmth of Joyce Ellis, who polished the many jagged edges.

. . . my new publisher, Warren Walsh of Emerald Books, for warmly embracing my work and creating a welcome place for me.

. . . my parents, Norman and Ethel, and my sister Nancy, for journeying with me in my own recovery process. I appreciate their willingness to examine our family rules and work to end our shame.

I especially want to thank the clients who trusted me enough to reveal their inner selves. Their courage and determination to grow and change has expanded my understanding of the dynamics of shame and recovery.

I also owe a great debt to my wife Lizz, whose commitment to excellence made this book possible. I thank her for the love and attention she gave to both the project and me.

PART ONE

SHAME
AND
FALLENNESS

CHAPTER 1

SHAME AND ADAM AND EVE

Ben has missed church services for several Sundays, and you are puzzled about it. For years he has been a regular usher at the 10:30 A.M. service, always present, always greeting you warmly, and always making sure you and your family are seated comfortably. His gracious hospitality and broad, warm smile constantly have helped you feel at home in your church.

As you open this morning's newspaper, your eyes jerk to a halt at the sight of Ben's photograph. The accompanying story is even more alarming. Ben has been arrested for misusing his position as a school counselor, for sexually abusing two girls from the local high school. You feel shocked and confused. You ask yourself, "How could Ben do such a terrible thing while being such a faithful servant to our church?"

How Can Good People Go Wrong?

Frank and Marlene have been married for nearly seventeen years. Their teenage children, Karin and Jack, are tall like their father and sensitive like their mother. One year apart in age, the two have been typical children—best friends one day, enemies the next. Frank has been a successful businessman all his life and

Marlene has been very active in her church. On the surface the family appears to be a textbook definition of the ideal family. Sadly, this picture-perfect family has been marred.

When Marlene was a girl, her family did not promote educational success. Her parents had not attended college, so she had few role models for academic achievement. Consequently, Marlene was a poor to average student, always considering herself one of the "dumb" kids in school. She had dreamed of college but never was able to enroll.

Upon marrying and becoming a mother, Marlene grew concerned about her children's academic life. She vowed that they would do better than she had and would go to college. To Marlene's joy, both Karin and Jack were good students, easily earning top grades. Things began to change, however, when Karin reached the eighth grade.

Inexplicably, Karin became disenchanted and lost all interest in school. As time progressed she spent an increasing amount of time watching television, especially music videos. Marlene became frantic. She imagined Karin dropping out of school, getting pregnant, or becoming involved with the drug crowd.

Marlene attempted to pressure Karin in every way she knew. She desperately wanted Karin back on track. When fighting with Karin proved unsuccessful, Marlene began arguing with Frank. Blaming him for Karin's behavior, she charged that his lack of discipline was at the root of Karin's problems.

The more Frank and Marlene argued, the more alienated Marlene felt from her family and the more panic she felt about Karin. She grew obsessed with the thought of Karin's life in ruin. Marlene had trouble thinking clearly and sleeping. At some moments her heart raced uncontrollably. As Marlene continually focused on fear over her daughter, she lost her ability to function at home. Her fear, ever expanding, had developed into full-blown panic attacks.

What caused both Ben and Marlene to act as they did? What derailed the lives of seemingly exemplary people? Unresolved shame. The Adam and Eve Complex.

Although these are only two examples of the many faces of shame, they show that even successful, popular, and seemingly "all-together" individuals may be plagued by shame issues. Yet there are common threads in their lifestyles:

1. Lack of genuinely knowing themselves.
2. Disconnectedness from their feelings.
3. Distorted personal boundaries.
4. Alienation from others.
5. Unmet needs.

Back to the Garden

I believe the answer to shame comes from an integration of psychological and theological concepts that I call the Adam and Eve Complex. Why the name? Because it all began in this very familiar story:

> *When the woman saw that the fruit of the tree was good for food and pleasing to the eye, and also desirable for gaining wisdom, she took some and ate it. She also gave some to her husband, who was with her, and he ate it. Then the eyes of both of them were opened, and they realized they were naked; so they sewed fig leaves together and made coverings for themselves.*
>
> *Then the man and his wife heard the sound of the LORD God as he was walking in the garden in the cool of the day, and they hid from the LORD God among the trees of the garden. But the LORD God called to the man, "Where are you?"*
>
> *He answered, "I heard you in the garden, and I was afraid because I was naked; so I hid."*
>
> *And he said, "Who told you that you were naked? Have you eaten from the tree that I commanded you not to eat from?"*
>
> *The man said, "The woman you put here with me—she gave me some fruit from the tree, and I ate it."*

> *Then the LORD God said to the woman, "What is this you have done?"*
>
> *The woman said, "The serpent deceived me, and I ate." (Genesis 3:6-13)*

Here is the beginning of shame, the tragedy of people hiding from God, themselves, and others. It has plagued human beings ever since. Capsulized in this brief account is the explanation of why each of us is born into a life of alienation.

Three principles emerge from the scriptural account of Adam and Eve. The principles that comprise the Adam and Eve Complex are defined by the faulty thoughts, protective actions, and deceptive lifestyle of each shame-based individual. I call these principles the tenets of shame.

The Tenets of Shame

Tenet One: Faulty Beliefs

The first tenet of shame reveals itself in three core beliefs commonly established in childhood.

1.   I am worthless and unacceptable to God, myself, and others.

2.   Others will abandon me. I must meet my own needs.

3.   Life will never get better, and I am helpless to change it.

Tenet Two: Protective Actions

The second tenet of shame specifies a set of actions or behaviors based on a fear of losing control, being discovered, and being rejected. This protective action is that of hiding from God, others, and self.

Tenet Three: Deceptive Lifestyle

Over time these beliefs and actions solidify in an adult lifestyle. This third tenet of shame consists of a lifestyle based on deception, blame, lies, and anger, which leave the person alienated and estranged from God, self, and others.

But what relevance do these tenets have for our lives? Recently shame has burst out of hiding. It has received increased attention on television, in newspapers, and in popular magazines. Despite this exposure, shame is a topic shrouded in mystery and misunderstanding because people usually associate it with embarrassing acts, personal failures, rejection, sexuality, secrets, or misdeeds.

The issue will gain clarity as we see that shame dates back to Adam and Eve and that it radically interfered with their (and our) spiritual and interpersonal relationships as well as their (and our) psychological well-being. Explained in its biblical context it becomes clear that shame leads to spiritual death as we, out of fear, retreat and hide from God. With shame there is no forgiveness, only anger, blame, betrayal, and despair. Consequently, we search to fill the spiritual vacuum, the sense of emptiness, loneliness, and alienation.

Shame-based people do not allow themselves to be vulnerable because they assume that neither God nor people can be reliable sources of support. They cover up painful memories, misbehavior, and such feelings as sadness, fear, hurt, and disappointment. In place of true intimacy and spiritual communion, shame-based persons engage in a variety of unhealthy relationships with substitutes—food, sex, chemicals, money, perfectionism, and abusive or self-destructive behaviors.

Thankfully, God has provided a way to freedom from shame, which is why *Looking Good Outside, Feeling Bad Inside* was written. Through this book we will gain a developmental understanding of shame by blending both psychological and spiritual viewpoints with the biblical story of Adam and Eve, thus realizing a historical perspective on the origins of shame. This new insight can benefit us immensely.

Insight alone, however, often is inadequate to bring about change. Change requires risk, courage, and despair over our present life. Therefore, the recovery process detailed in this book requires deep inner searching and an honest quest for truth about who we really are. Denial and hiding of weaknesses and blemishes are central to shame. These behaviors must be exposed to the light of truth, replete with the raw feelings that attend them.

The Path of Recovery

The fruit of a shame-based life may include addictive, abusive, or indulgent behavior. Breaking the grip of such behaviors is not something to be taken lightly. Usually change begins only after some influence, possibly a cataclysmic personal event (which I call an "earthquake") supplies the motivation and accountability. Because of human nature, most people do not change unless the leverage of significant pain drives them to the realization that unless they do something drastic and soon, they may lose everything. Therefore, I understand and appreciate the serious task of the reader, whether you be the person seeking recovery, a concerned family member or friend, a pastor, a pastoral caregiver, or a helping professional.

I have written this book as a guide for a person in the recovery process. Recovery is no easy task. It requires a safe, supportive environment so we can freely explore and release the secrets and shame that have bound us. However, no one can change in isolation. With understanding supporters nearby and by applying the principles in this book we can overcome the shame that has nearly destroyed us.

The remainder of the first part of this book outlines the individual characteristics of the shame-based individual, describing the developmental journey in detail. The first several chapters may seem somewhat heavy and uncomfortable to read. Some of the case studies may feel too close to home. On the other hand, while a particular case history may not seem to apply at first, a later reading may reveal amazing similarities to your own predicament. Often people with shame do not want to see what is painful or distressing, but in fact that is a necessary part of the process. Answers and healing lie ahead if we apply the principles outlined.

The journey of Part One uncovers the beliefs we learn in infancy and childhood; the unique set of behavior patterns that emerge in adolescence; and the adult lifestyle characterized by denial, deception, and alienation. These developments will, of course, be examined in light of the Adam and Eve Complex.

In Part Two we explore a psychological and spiritual road to recovery. Hope and healing may come in unexpected ways! We must begin by uncovering the Adam and Eve belief system and breaking the dominance of unhealthy family rules. Repressed emotional pain may surface, requiring a grieving process. At this point we can undertake new risks to test whether or not others really will abandon us. In a new, deeper way we are likely to discover the true meaning of God's gift of grace. Then we can receive genuine support as our self-protective wall crumbles and our real selves can be known.

In Part Three the old Adam and Eve beliefs are replaced with new grace-full beliefs. Our feelings of worthlessness are changed to feelings of acceptance, abandonment to trust, and helplessness to empowerment. Embodying this transformation is a new lifestyle—relating without shame. Having a genuine, intimate, and loving relationship with God, others, and ourselves is truly possible: We can live free of shame.

Assessing Our Shame

It is not easy to assess our shame. Part of this difficulty lies in the fact that the more shame we have, the greater our denial will be. Therefore I have designed the Shame Indicator, a self-assessment tool that helps identify the level of our shame. As self-assessment is meant to be constructive and confidential, we must be committed to answering the questions honestly and thoughtfully in order to gain an accurate appraisal of our shame. The resulting information can then guide us in recovery.

SHAME INDICATOR:

*A Self-Assessment Profile of Shame**

Instructions: Respond to each question by circling either True or False. When in doubt, base your response on the answer that appears most correct.

* This is a nonscientific instrument intended solely as an informational device.

1. I have been told that I have poor eye contact, slump my shoulders, or blush easily.　　TRUE　FALSE

2. I am more perfectionistic than I would like to be.　　TRUE　FALSE

3. I get defensive when others criticize me.　　TRUE　FALSE

4. It is relatively easy for me to criticize members of my family, people at work or school, God, or myself.　　TRUE　FALSE

5. I don't accept compliments well.　　TRUE　FALSE

6. When I'm lost I find it difficult to ask for directions or help from others.　　TRUE　FALSE

7. When I make mistakes I feel bad for hours, even days.　　TRUE　FALSE

8. I find it difficult to trust that others will meet my needs.　　TRUE　FALSE

9. When things go wrong I have a hard time accepting blame.　　TRUE　FALSE

10. I cannot talk to my friends and family about my fears and disappointments.　　TRUE　FALSE

11. I feel down, hopeless, and overwhelmed a good deal of the time.　　TRUE　FALSE

12. I feel that I get angrier or angry more often than most people.　　TRUE　FALSE

13. I find it hard to rest or relax without feeling guilty.　　TRUE　FALSE

14. I was teased and called names when I was young.　　TRUE　FALSE

15. I rarely reveal my feelings.　　TRUE　FALSE

16. If someone does me a favor, I worry about having to return it.　　TRUE　FALSE

17. I am sure I have addictive qualities in my
    personality.   TRUE   FALSE

18. I have difficulty holding a job or maintaining
    a friendship for a long period of time.   TRUE   FALSE

19. As a child I felt neglected or abused.   TRUE   FALSE

20. I have a hard time believing that God can
    fully love and accept me.   TRUE   FALSE

21. I never allow myself to get angry.   TRUE   FALSE

22. My family of origin did not encourage or
    nurture my self-worth.   TRUE   FALSE

23. I have great difficulty getting close to peo-
    ple.   TRUE   FALSE

24. I have secrets that would surprise and shock
    others.   TRUE   FALSE

25. I feel embarrassed or humiliated by certain
    things from my past.   TRUE   FALSE

26. Growing up I received little or no support or
    praise for my accomplishments.   TRUE   FALSE

27. I have trouble praying to God after I do
    something wrong.   TRUE   FALSE

28. When with my family of origin, I rarely feel
    as if I'm treated as an adult.   TRUE   FALSE

29. I feel things must be done my way.   TRUE   FALSE

30. I take myself too seriously.   TRUE   FALSE

Scoring: Calculate the score by assigning one point to each TRUE response, then adding all of the points.

SCORE: _19_

Interpreting your Shame Indicator score:

Score	Level of Shame
0-9	Limited
10-15	Moderate
15 or more	Significant

According to this informal test, the higher the score, the greater our probable level of shame. In contrast, the lower the score, the less our shame. However, a low score also could indicate denial. Only by reading on and applying the concepts of the Adam and Eve Complex will we come to fully recognize the depth of our shame and finally be able to find healing. The secrets of how to more deeply love ourselves, others, and God are ahead.

CHAPTER 2

CHILDHOOD AND SHAME

Mike was the kind of citizen any community would be proud to have. An ambulance attendant for a moderate-size hospital in the Midwest, Mike had received several commendations for his heroic, lifesaving efforts. He attended church regularly and often was sought out as a volunteer because of his cooperative nature. But something changed in the life of this active, caring man. Recently, after battling several bouts of severe depression, Mike attempted suicide.

In large part Mike's suicide attempt was triggered by his wife's sudden death. Married for barely a year, Linda was diagnosed with a fast-growing cancer and survived only a few months. Mike's grief provoked feelings of abandonment and an overwhelming sense of worthlessness—emotions that were not new to him.

Mike grew up in the Colorado mountains where his father, John, worked long hours as a machinist. John was an extremely passive man. On the other hand, his wife, Ann, was hostile and abusive, particularly toward Mike. Having been physically abused by her father, a man known to have had several affairs, Ann had grown to distrust and deeply resent men. She vented much of her anger on her children. And her only son, Mike, received the brunt of it.

Daily Mike's mother told him what a terrible child he was. As if that were not vicious enough, she would add, "You're just too much to handle. Sometimes I feel like the only way out is to kill myself. Don't be surprised if you come home from school someday and find me lying in a pool of blood."

Horribly burdened by her frequent threat, Mike went to school each day with terrible, aching knots in his stomach, afraid his mother would be dead when he returned.

It might be easy to surmise that Mike's miserable childhood was the reason for his depression. However, that is not the premise of this book. Even Mike realized the futility in such a conclusion. Childhood is not the cause of shame-based living. It is, however, a beginning point for understanding how a shame-based identity is formed.

Karen Horney, a prominent psychologist in the early 1900s, commented on such experiences: "If a child is exposed to such an unfavorable environment it will develop an insidiously increasing, all-pervading feeling of being lonely and helpless in a hostile world."[1] Hurtful, negative messages during childhood nourish the development of shame-based core beliefs. In turn these beliefs are fertile soil for psychological disorders, addictions, and estrangement from God, others, and even self.

How Belief Systems Develop

A person's belief systems, formed in childhood, are shaped by three distinct sets of factors. First are the *biological factors* that influence the child. Certainly a child born with mental impairments because of the mother's cocaine addiction will have a very different life than the exceptionally bright child of healthy, physically normal parents.

Second are *environmental factors*—circumstances and conditions that make up the child's surroundings, such as a middle-class neighborhood, a single parent, or alcoholic parents. As with biological factors, the child has no control over these influences.

Third are *interpretative factors*. These, the central theme of this book, are the child's interpretations of life events. These interpretations, and their resultant belief system, supply the keys to understanding a person's behavior.

Alfred Adler, one of the forefathers of modern psychology, offered theories about these interpretive factors that are both pragmatic and highly consistent with scriptural teaching. Adler believed that we all come into the world feeling small and inferior. These inferior feelings are justified because a baby or child is a small, helpless creature who depends on others for survival. The child looks to significant caregivers for insight on how to fit in or belong in the world.

From an Adlerian view, actual life experiences do not form the child's personality; rather, the child's *interpretations* of those events make the difference. For example, consider how differently people respond to an identical event, such as a divorce. Some, for instance, would view the impending divorce as a terrible sin and feel overwhelmed with guilt; others would see it as a relief; and still others would regard at it as an unfortunate event but have relatively few feelings. The event, divorce, would be the same in each case, yet the feelings about the event would be unique to each person, directly reflecting each person's belief system. Therefore, interpretations and belief systems, not just life experiences, are vitally important.

Thousands of years before Adler proposed his concepts, the Bible said much the same thing: "For as he thinketh in his heart, so is he" (Proverbs 23:7, AV). William Backus and Marie Chapian, in their popular book *Telling Yourself the Truth*, confirm this, noting that "the Bible solidly teaches that man's feelings, passions and behavior are subject to and conditioned by the way he thinks."[2]

Because children are wonderful observers but poor interpreters, they can develop mistaken ideas about self and the world around them. This "private logic" comprises a set of attitudes that govern how people size up the world, including their own self-concept.

If, for example, children believe they are unwanted, they may unconsciously try to prove it by demonstrating how unworthy they are of their parents' love. Such children may cry and whine endlessly or perhaps throw tantrums or smash toys. Their beliefs, largely subconscious, govern how they respond to the environment.

Each child thus constructs a belief system based in part on reality and in part on faulty interpretations. If children become shame-based adults they have a belief system that says they are deficient, unacceptable, and helpless to change their predicament.

The Adam and Eve Complex and the Child

As explained in the first chapter, the Adam and Eve Complex, based on Genesis, chapter three, is comprised of three key tenets of shame. The first tenet is the faulty belief system developed in childhood. The second tenet is the pattern of protective actions that evolve from the child's psychological belief system. The third tenet is a deceptive lifestyle, the unique identity that characterizes the fallen human condition that betrays a shame-based individual.

Tenet One: Faulty Beliefs

Faulty belief number one: "I am worthless and unacceptable to God, myself, and others."

After eating the forbidden fruit, Adam and Eve realized they were naked and they attempted to cover themselves. This reaction to their nakedness can be described as shame. If we analyze their actions from a psychological standpoint, they likely believed that they no longer were acceptable, lovable, or pleasing in the eyes of God.

These same beliefs are commonly seen in children when they make mistakes or do wrongful acts. They misinterpret their parents' response, believing that they, themselves, are bad or worthless rather than seeing their actions as bad.

Children who believe they have lost all value will develop an Adam and Eve belief system. Over time they may fall prey to a great deal of unhappiness. As adults, they may be susceptible to a host of problems, such as abuse, addiction, or relationship failures. Ultimately they will feel a strong sense of alienation from God, from others, and even from self.

When Mike, the ambulance attendant, was a child, his major reference point for self-worth was his mother's statements. Because she said he was bad, Mike interpreted her statements to mean that the whole world viewed him as worthless, unacceptable, and displeasing. He did not understand that the real issue was his behavior (and his mother's dysfunctional childhood), not his worth as a person.

In addition, as a child Mike could not challenge or question his mother's statements for fear of reprisal. The shaming and belittling messages he internalized from her became part of his private logic. Therefore, when Mike's wife died he instinctively reverted to those early childhood beliefs, viewing himself as obviously unlovable and unacceptable. These faulty thoughts hurled him into extreme depression.

How can we discover what our private logic is? One effective method is to recall our earliest childhood memories, preferably those before age six. These memories are important because they provide clues about how we viewed ourselves and our world as our personality was being shaped. While we have thousands of memories, usually we remember only those few that are the most significant or meaningful for us. Within these memories lay the core beliefs of the Adam and Eve Complex.

David is a Christian with deep faith, and his memories clearly reveal his private logic. One of his most vivid recollections is that of taking a boat ride with his family to see a magnificent dam.

Upon arriving, the boat was tied to the dock, and David's family started to disembark. But David sat paralyzed, afraid to get out. A large crowd stood looking at the dam, and David instantly assumed that he would have to push his way through the crowd. Afraid of getting lost or being stranded by his parents, he froze with fear, unable to summon the courage to move. David's parents misjudged his behavior as stubbornness and left him in the boat alone. David felt abandoned.

When his father returned, David was crying, his face swollen with tears. Instead of trying to console his son, the man chided, "Stop your stupid crying." David felt even more belittled. He felt his father didn't care for him.

What is significant in this story is not the event itself—for we all have disappointments—but David's interpretations, his private logic. David believed that no one cared about him, that his needs were unimportant, and that he was helpless to change the circumstances. This was self-deception. In reality David had, out of fear, chosen not to see the dam. Even though his dad accused him of being stupid, he was not. David simply was a frightened child needing reassurance.

Thirty years later David's private logic remains unchanged, and he can recall graphically the details of the boat ride, including his feelings. Now chemically dependent, David still views himself as worthless and unimportant.

Faulty belief number two: "Others will abandon me. I therefore must meet my own needs."

For Adam and Eve there was no return, either to their wondrous home in the Garden of Eden or to the unhindered intimacy they once enjoyed with God. Their lives and world were now forever marred because God's perfect way had been violated. The world no longer was under their control. The animals, the plants, the soil itself now threatened their survival.

In a similar way, severed relationships with parents or significant caregivers severely affect children. The child interprets the loss through death, divorce, chemical dependency, or a debilitating illness as, "I've been abandoned forever."

As a child Mike came to believe that his mother was undependable. He could not even trust her to be alive when he came home from school. For any child, similar life experiences may give rise to feelings of rejection and abandonment, resulting in the development of an attitude of distrust. Believing that others will reject, abandon, shame, or harm them, the child steadfastly stays on the defense, armoring all signs of weakness.

This was also Gail's experience. Gail's father died when she was in the third grade, and her mother responded to the death by taking sedatives, eventually becoming addicted. A thin, spindly child, Gail felt rejected, alone, and terribly scared.

Believing she had been abandoned forever by both parents, she put up an aggressive facade. She wanted no one to know how scared and fragile she really felt. Constantly fearful of being alone or of being teased or criticized, Gail would fight with anyone who dared taunt her. On several occasions her actions sent youngsters to the school nurse's office with bloody noses or blackened eyes.

Gail's brother reinforced her belief that she had been abandoned. Because they had no father, her brother threatened that if Gail did anything wrong, she would end up in an orphanage. Obviously Gail had done nothing to warrant such severe treatment, but at the age of eight she did not understand this. Her aggressive way of hiding her fear, pain, and hurt only fostered greater feelings of shame and further reinforced her feelings of abandonment.

If people believe they will be abandoned, their natural reaction is to stop depending on others. This is how Adam and Eve reacted. God had provided for all of their wants and needs as long as they lived obediently in the garden. Everything was theirs to enjoy—except one tree. After eating the forbidden fruit they gained a new perspective of their nakedness, then chose to take matters into their own hands by clothing themselves. Adam and Eve thus turned further away from God.

Just as Adam and Eve stopped depending on God, the child with a core belief that says, "Others will abandon me, so I must meet my own needs" stops relying on other people. The child actively avoids the risk of rejection and thus declines the help, support, and love of others.

Deep within, the child believes, "I can't trust others to support my emotional needs. I can count only on myself." This manifests itself in an unwillingness to ask for help and a refusal to cooperate with other children. The child becomes a "loner," withdrawing from others.

The child's belief, "I can count only on myself," is false pride, an infatuation with one's self-image. This pride rejects any need for God, parents, or other people. Such children believe they can be self-sufficient.

False pride results in emotional deprivation; it is impossible for a young child to be self-sufficient. Rather than ask for support, help, or encouragement, such children turn to things to meet their needs. Toys, pets, or computer games become the total focus. These children also begin to depersonalize others, viewing people in terms of "what can they give to 'me'?" Such children may act extremely selfish and cruel, showing no signs of remorse afterward. As this cyclic pattern of behavior is established, these children become certain they really are bad, unacceptable, and unlovable.

Faulty belief number three: "Life will never get better, and I am helpless to change it."

A child who is treated badly or who interprets the world as hostile and threatening fails to mature adequately. For example, after being abused frequently by a parent, the child will tend to associate abusive behaviors with that parent. Anytime the parent is present that child will expect to be abused. Such abusive treatment distorts the child's sense of time. A day or a week becomes an eternity and the child assumes that nothing will ever change for the better.

Just as Adam and Eve were expelled from the Garden of Eden

forever, children may believe that lack of self-worth and emotional deprivation will last forever. Often this leads to deep-seated depression and a helplessness that says, "Nothing can be done to change my life."

To compensate for the depression, again these children may develop a false pride that says, "I can meet all my own needs." Though such self-talk can insulate from the pain temporarily, such a defense prevents the healing of emotional wounds. It allows no one to give support. Consequently such children need more and more defensive walls to protect their bruised selves.

Tenet Two: Protective Actions

After Adam and Eve ate the fruit, they hid from God. This reaction likely was prompted by fear of punishment or other consequences for their disobedience. By the age of three or four, children often hide when they have done something wrong because they fear their parents' reaction. Children understand that there are rules, but their motto simply becomes, "Don't get caught." While normal children outgrow this attitude, the shame-based person unconsciously retains it into adulthood.

In order to live by the credo, "Don't get caught," children attempt to control life, reasoning that by doing so, life will not control them. They strive to get their own way by manipulating and conning others because they are convinced that other people wouldn't take the side of a child.

We can see this striving for control throughout childhood, especially when a mother laments, "As soon as I tell her what to do, she does just the opposite!" Protective actions also may include constant tardiness, defiance of rules, and disrespect of authority.

Such is the case with Bruce. At the tender age of seven, Bruce is a world-class con artist who skillfully weasels his parents, siblings, and teachers into giving him his way. Bruce never takes no for an answer. When he fails to study for a test at school, he suddenly becomes so sick he can't get out of bed; yet the minute the bus has left he sits vacant-eyed in front of the television, munching chocolate chip cookies. Even simple events, such as taking a bath, cleaning his room, or even eating meals, become nightmares for his parents, who can't get him to cooperate.

An opposite hiding strategy may be an overconscientious attitude. These children must be liked at all costs and therefore become watchful of others, anticipating their every need. Such children may behave as puppets, trained to please other people's slightest whims. In essence they become chameleons, changing color with every circumstance. Yet even after sacrificing to meet everyone else's needs, they still feel unacceptable and deficient. They dare not show anyone their true identity and feel they cannot be loved for who they really are.

As these children attempt to control life to avoid getting caught, they may become filled with fear, dread, anxiety, and apprehension. Uncertain about trusting others, they must struggle to control anything and everything around them. Consequently a tremendous fear of losing physical and psychological control overwhelms them.

Fear of losing physical control may mean being terrified by their own anger and rage. These children may view themselves as having superhuman power to destroy others. This can give rise to fears that in a fight they easily might kill an opponent with one good punch. In addition, they may fear situations in which they might be physically vulnerable. Going to the doctor or dentist may be traumatic because they must risk surrendering to another person.

For children, fear of losing psychological control is often the terror of being rejected, laughed at, criticized, or belittled. They may become hypersensitive to even the slightest glance of disapproval. In response they alienate themselves from potential playmates. They cannot afford to be anyone's friend. They may behave aggressively by fighting, breaking school rules, or talking back to people in authority. These actions are self-protective measures, for even the slightest criticism must be stopped at all costs.

Children who perceive the world as a threat and people as enemies can be full of hostility. The feelings may be so intense that these children have great difficulty releasing all of their pent-up energy. Such children may appear hyperactive and even have periods of insomnia.

These children also may think they can increase their own estimation of self-worth by making others feel inferior. They may taunt other children and engage in hurtful games. Who hasn't heard a child call, "Look, look!" then mock with, "I made you look, Dummy!"? Children often try to appear smarter and superior at someone else's expense.

Controlling children view the world as a hostile jungle. In order to survive they feel they must be the aggressor, unable to receive gifts of kindness, love, and support from God or others. These children cannot let down their guard.

Tenet Three: Deceptive Lifestyle

Two of history's most famous excuses come from the Garden of Eden: "I did nothing wrong; it's Eve's fault" and "The serpent made me do it." By blaming others, shame-based people divert attention away from themselves. In effect they are saying, "Don't look at me, you might find that I am deficient, needy, or worse, accountable for my actions."

Shame-based children fail to develop an internal sense of right or wrong. To them, "wrong" behavior is getting caught. Any other action is acceptable and right. They lack the capacity to judge their own actions accurately because they spend their lives hiding from the truth.

The most effective way to hide is to blame others or to blame external circumstances. Shame-based students caught stealing test answers from someone else's paper might retort, "If the stupid teacher hadn't been watching me I wouldn't have gotten caught cheating, and everything would be just fine." They interpret the problem to be the teacher rather than their own act of cheating.

These children cultivate a pattern of lying, deception, and blaming to deal with peers, playmates, and parents. This pattern becomes the foundation for an adult lifestyle. Such people learn how to defend themselves in a game in which high stakes demand self-protection and diversion.

By holding on to a faulty belief system children become emotionally bankrupt, with few effective skills or methods for achieving genuine intimacy. Mistakenly believing that relationships are too risky, they admit to needing no one. It is too likely that others will reject them, shame them, and leave them worse off than before.

As the Adam and Eve Complex develops, shame-based children fail to give others a chance to provide love and support. They miss almost all opportunities to empathize with others because their attitude toward the world is so hostile. With few if any genuine friendships, they often turn to the immediate gratification offered by food, chemicals, sex, or other substitutes. These substitutes nourish, though only temporarily, the primitive, basic emotional needs that desperately cry out to be satisfied.

Summary

The Adam and Eve Complex represents a set of beliefs and behaviors learned in childhood that later develop into an adult lifestyle. Central to this belief system are interpretations about life. Young, impressionable children may capsulize their beliefs this way: "I am unacceptable and worthless. I can depend only on myself. Nothing will ever change." They may demonstrate their interpretations through false pride, attempting either to control the environment or to be overresponsible. They also may use blame to avoid accountability.

Unable to control others or the environment, children with an Adam and Eve Complex experience anxiety, fear, and dread. Behavior takes the form of hostility, avoidance, or distancing. No one can get close to a person who is consumed by feelings of shame. As the child moves into adolescence, a shame-based lifestyle begins to emerge.

Questions to Ask Myself

1. What are my earliest memories and the feelings that accompany them? Did I interpret any of those events as signs that I had little value, that I could not count on others, or that I was helpless to change my life?

2. What events in my childhood were particularly shameful?

3. What traumatic losses did I experience as a child?

4. In what ways did my parents show me that I was loved, valued, and accepted?

5. What one or two people was I closest to as a child? How did these relationships affect my self-worth?

[1]Karen Horney, *Neurosis and Human Growth* (New York: Norton, 1950), 89.

[2]William Backus and Marie Chapian, *Telling Yourself the Truth* (Minneapolis: Bethany House, 1980), 16.

CHAPTER 3

ADOLESCENCE AND SHAME

Vivacious and beautiful, fifteen-year-old Tiffany appeared the ideal teenager. She played the piano and alto saxophone. She loved math. As for a career, she hoped to become a lawyer, a job well-suited to her strong disposition. Yet something suddenly changed. Her mother began noticing that Tiffany seemed withdrawn, often retreating to her bedroom, acting distant and aloof from both friends and family.

After Tiffany missed several get-togethers with her best friends and began refusing to join the family at mealtimes, her mother confronted her.

"What's wrong, Tiffany?" she asked.

"Nothing!" Tiffany snapped. She broke into tears and then uncontrollable sobs. "Oh, Mom," she cried, "it's too terrible to say."

"Please, Tiffany," her mother begged, "I can't help unless you tell me what's happened to you. You know how much I love you. Please tell me what's been bothering you."

"I'm so fat, no one talks to me anymore."

Her mother was incredulous. "Tiffany, you're not fat. You couldn't even weigh one hundred pounds. In fact, you look thin."

"Well, I am fat," Tiffany answered softly. "And the only way I'll be popular is to be thin. If I gain any more weight, I'll never have any friends. I have to get thin—" She hesitated. "And throwing up after I eat is the only thing I can do."

Hardly able to believe Tiffany's words, her mother felt stunned and sickened, all at once. Her precious, vulnerable princess had become bulimic. Because of shame.

No one totally escapes shame in adolescence. Yet the child whose private logic says, "I am unacceptable, alone, and helpless," often will begin displaying psychological symptoms or have significant relationship conflicts. This was true for Tiffany, and it is common among other shame-based adolescents.

A person's behavior is a direct outcome of attitudes. During childhood and adolescence the relationships formed with parents, playmates, and teachers, the exposure to the world gained through the media, and even the interaction one has with pets and animals help form an individualized set of attitudes. From this set of attitudes emerge values about self and life. Unfortunately, many people's values are based on their Adam and Eve Complex.

Sexuality: Fertile Ground for Shame

Adolescence is a time of discovery. New impulses, feelings, and urges bombard developing young people. Their sense of self, now familiar, drastically changes. They soon realize that adulthood is beckoning. Seemingly overnight they outgrow every pair of jeans in the closet, feel sexually aroused, and undergo physical changes such as sprouting body hair and a maturing body shape. How they cope with these changes is determined largely by attitudes.

In Steve's case unhealthy attitudes were his downfall. As a young child Steve embraced the belief system of the Adam and Eve Complex. With a shock of bright red hair, he was a younger version of his Irish father, Patrick. This resemblance unconsciously irritated Steve's mother, for Patrick had abandoned the family for another woman, leaving the mother to raise Steve and his older brother on her own.

Whether because of her childhood training or because of her husband's unfaithfulness, Steve's mother taught her sons that all sex was sinful. Therefore, by the time Steve reached adolescence he believed that any sexual feeling or behavior was wrong and that masturbating was a filthy, deeply perverse act. During his early adolescence Steve tried desperately to contain any and all sexual thoughts.

The fact that his brother Jim seemed to show no sexual responsibility (resulting in a pregnancy) only added to Steve's discomfort. Steve witnessed the hardship and shame his eighteen-year-old brother's behavior brought to the family and the huge burden it placed on his mother. Yet his brother seemed untroubled by the matter.

As his body began to feel the twinges of adolescent sexual energy, Steve found himself locked in a cognitive conflict: he believed sex was wrong, dirty, and sinful, yet he could not stop the sexual thoughts and ideas that entered his mind. He constantly felt shameful, burdened with the belief that he was doomed to hell.

Over time Steve became increasingly tormented by the fear of being rejected both by his mother and by God. Feeling very lonely, like many other adolescents, Steve discovered masturbation. Typically, he gained pleasure from masturbating, yet each episode brought renewed self-disgust and contempt.

Adolescents usually fail to develop a comprehensive understanding of God's purpose for sexuality. They may read the verse, "But I tell you that anyone who looks at a woman lustfully has already committed adultery with her in his heart," (Matthew 5:28) and with little other instruction or knowledge may surmise that God condemns all sexual behaviors and feelings, that it is wrong even to feel attraction toward someone of the opposite sex. As a result these adolescents learn the DON'TS but not the DOs of healthy sexual behavior.

In an attempt to feel accepted by God, adolescents with an Adam and Eve Complex may try to repress all sexual feelings and thoughts. When unable to do so they may secretly seek out a pornographic magazine, masturbate, or even have sexual relations with another adolescent, male or female. Such clandestine behaviors often give rise to more intense sexual fantasies and, consequently, even greater feelings of shame and spiritual condemnation. Amid such turmoil such adolescents lack role models with whom they can discuss sexual feelings.

For Steve, the sexual upheaval in his body left him feeling rejected and abandoned by both parents. His father had left home when Steve was only three years old, so Steve had little memory of him. And because the strong resemblance between father and son distressed Steve's mother, she often lashed out at Steve with anger and frustration that actually were directed at the boy's father. Steve grew up believing the message, "Life will never get better, and I am helpless to change it."

Entwined with Steve's belief was a sense of anger at his mother for her rigid and overprotective behavior. During his junior high school years she refused to let him join the wrestling team because she deemed wrestling a rough and dangerous sport. She also monitored all of his telephone calls to make certain he did not talk to friends she had blacklisted.

As he reached late adolescence Steve's anger at his mother began to fuel his sexual fantasies. More and more his fantasies were of dominating or overpowering women. Unconsciously these fantasies were a way to get back at his mother and give Steve a sense of control.

As a result, Steve's fantasies and sexual behaviors incited even stronger feelings of shame and spiritual condemnation. He found himself in a vicious circle: he felt that his sexual behaviors made him unacceptable to God, but masturbation seemed to be his only relief from the misery of shame. He was trapped in a continual cycle of temporary relief and compounding shame.

Shame and Hiding

Sexual maturation is central to a successful adolescence. Unfortunately, an adolescent is very vulnerable, both spiritually and psychologically, so their sexual feelings and behaviors are extremely susceptible to shame. This shame, of course, directly reinforces the core beliefs of the Adam and Eve Complex. Thus, holding on to the Adam and Eve Complex only produces disillusionment, despair, and depression in the adolescent.

In order to hide the pain, the adolescent develops a number of behavior patterns to conceal the Adam and Eve belief system—much like layers of an onion. However, just as a wound sealed from the air will not heal quickly, shame, as an infecting wound, does not heal when heavily bandaged.

In order to more fully understand the hiding aspect of shame we need to consider again the story of Adam and Eve.

When the woman saw that the fruit of the tree was good for food and pleasing to the eye, and also desirable for gaining wisdom, she took some and ate it. She also gave some to her husband, who was with her, and he ate it. Then the eyes of both of them were opened, and they realized they were naked; so they sewed fig leaves together and made coverings for themselves.

Then the man and his wife heard the sound of the LORD God as he was walking in the garden in the cool of the day, and they hid from the LORD God among the trees of the garden. (Genesis 3:6-8)

Adam and Eve's disobedience and their ensuing shame exposed their vulnerabilities and naked spirits and bodies before God. These feelings made Adam and Eve uncomfortable with the appearance of their unclothed bodies. They feared God's rejection and no longer experienced the joy they had known when communing with him in the Garden of Eden.

But the LORD God called to the man, "Where are you?"

He answered, "I heard you in the garden, and I was afraid because I was naked; so I hid." (Genesis 3:9-10)

Instead of joyously anticipating seeing God and communing with him, they hid. In that moment of hiding Adam and Eve had supplanted love and acceptance with fear and doubt.

Shame had no part in God's original plan for humankind. Instead of enhancing our relationship with him, it prevents us from accepting God's love and the love of others. Shame causes us to disregard who we are and what God made us to be. It also impedes our ability to mend relationships. Instead of honestly admitting our shortcomings, we lie and run from our responsibilities.

Obviously, shame is unhealthy. However, often it is misunderstood. Many people confuse shame with its healthy counterpart—guilt. The following chart compares these two concepts and the dynamics of each.

Guilt versus Shame

Guilt	Shame
The principle focus is on specific behaviors.	The principle focus is on the person.
"You didn't make the bed."	"How could you be such a dumb jerk?"
"You were supposed to take out the garbage."	"You're good for nothing!"
"I was late for work again."	"I'm so stupid!"
Forgiveness and resolution are possible. Accepting forgiveness and adopting new behaviors (making the bed, taking out the garbage, and being on time) remove guilt.	Forgiveness and resolution are impossible. At issue is one's defectiveness, which cannot be changed. Therefore, shame cannot be removed.
The object of guilt is to act responsibly.	The object of shame is to blame and punish.
Typically, guilt is the result of not living up to the standards we believe in and adopt as our own.	Typically, shame is the result of not living up to the standards other people impose on us.
Guilt can be healthy, reminding us of what is right and moral without attacking our self-esteem.	Shame is unhealthy, damaging our spirit, hindering change, and alienating us from others.

At the heart of the Adam and Eve Complex are people who have come to believe they are bad, deficient, and unlovable. Because shame precludes forgiveness, shame-based people lose the courage to believe that others would willingly support and accept them.

In the case of an adolescent shame supports a pattern of learned helplessness that says, "Why even ask for help or understanding? I can't trust anyone to give it to me anyway." Instead of relying on God, parents, friends, or siblings to meet emotional needs, the adolescent may turn to drugs, sex, food, or even performance (for example, scholastic or athletic achievement) as a principal source of good feelings.

From a biblical perspective I believe such behavior is idolatry, as these means of achieving acceptance or love become substitute gods. They reflect the belief, "I can't really trust God to fill me up or make me feel okay. I can trust only drugs (or sex, or good grades) to do it."

The Adolescent's Psychological Belief System

Tenet One: Faulty Beliefs

Faulty belief number one: "I am worthless and unacceptable to God, myself, and others."

Internal belief systems are bolstered by external events. When children believe they are worthless and unacceptable to God, self, and others, this belief not only continues into adolescence, it is reinforced—particularly in school. Because adolescent life centers around school activities, their belief in their own worthlessness affects both academic progress and the development of peer relationships. If convinced they have little value they will be unable to make a commitment to learning and to developing friendships with others who treat them respectfully.

In the academic realm a learning disability or the label of "slow learner" is common for adolescents with an Adam and Eve Complex. Unfortunately, such a handicap only multiplies their feelings of low self-worth. In addition to earning poor grades, these adolescents may also frequently find themselves in trouble for such behavior problems as abusive language, vandalism, or truancy.

Sadly, those in authority often deal with the behavior by accentuating the adolescents' negative rather than positive attributes, telling them they are stupid, no good, or troublemakers. Parents may impose harsh punishment, but sometimes they become so exasperated that they let inappropriate behaviors slide. Many parents simply become too tired to deal with it all. Inconsistent parenting reinforces what these young people already believe is most important: Don't get caught.

For shame-based people, the parent-child bond that was damaged during childhood is never allowed to heal during adolescence. If death, divorce, alcoholism, or some other major family stressor occurs during this period, the wedge between parent and child grows even wider.

Thus, adolescents who have developed an Adam and Eve Complex believe that no one really cares about them and that life is grossly unfair. These beliefs intensify their anger and depression. As a result they may abandon parental and societal values and embrace a set of values based on the distorted Adam and Eve belief system adopted in childhood.

Sixteen-year-old Marilyn did just that. The daughter of wealthy parents, Marilyn horrified her family by leaving home and moving in with her boyfriend, a man ten years her senior. Marilyn defended her action by claiming that this way she would have some stability and not be subjected to moving each time her father's job demanded it. (Her father was a vice president for a large company, and business had taken them from one large city to the next.) Marilyn felt that if her father really had cared about her, he would not have made the family move so often. She craved attention and a "normal" life. Her life seemed so unfair. Angry at her parents, Marilyn chose a set of values directly opposite those of her parents.

Continuing in their belief that "I am worthless and unacceptable to God, myself, and others," adolescents begin to view others in the same light (that others are equally worthless and unacceptable). This attitude is fostered by these children's extreme anger and discouragement. Because they have no adequate bond with parents or other people, their attitude provides a way to retaliate, to lash out at their parents and at the world.

Most often shame-based adolescents act out their pain in two ways—by withdrawing or by retreating into nonconformity.

Some adolescents respond to their pain by withdrawing from others and isolating themselves. Relying on illicit drugs and alcohol, masturbation, television viewing, food, or other external means allows them to escape from their feelings of being alone and unlovable.

Others act out their pain by retreating into nonconformity. Rules have little value to those who don't care what their parents or teachers say. "After all," the adolescent may reason, "they don't accept me anyway." Consequently, shame-based adolescents have few internal rules or limits on personal behavior. They don't care what others think. They do whatever they want.

In either case a self-fulfilling prophecy results in:

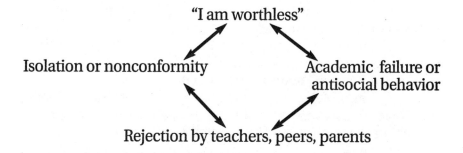

"I am worthless"

Isolation or nonconformity

Academic failure or antisocial behavior

Rejection by teachers, peers, parents

Faulty belief number two: "Others will abandon me. I therefore must meet my own needs."

As the above diagram portrays, these adolescents unwittingly participate in a self-fulfilling prophecy that causes others to reject and leave them. By acting rudely or ignoring other people's attempts to befriend them, they close the door to genuine friendship or intimacy. Thus, they become further alienated from healthy peers and instead align themselves with other adolescents who do not fit in.

In order to deal with this pain, the false pride nurtured in childhood drives its roots deeper, further reinforced by the adolescent belief that "I don't need anyone. I can take care of myself." Because these young people are survivors, they have learned to distrust others and tune out their real feelings. Psychologically they have numbed all emotions by discounting fear, pain, loneliness, and unhappiness.

That is just what Melissa did. Melissa was a victim of economic crisis. While growing up she and her family lived on a farm in the Midwest. Her father, Sam, was a farmer, as his father had been. While farm life had provided Sam's father with a good living, it was not so generous to Sam. After several years of crop failure, most of the property was sold so that the family could pay its debts. Sam went into a tailspin of depression. Although he and his wife tried their best to keep the family together, they eventually divorced. Melissa was sent to live with her maternal grandparents.

These tragic events supported Melissa's Adam and Eve belief of "Others will abandon me." She responded predictably. First, she isolated herself. Because of her passion for mystery books, when she felt alone and frightened—which was often—she would retreat and escape from the world by reading book after book.

Second, Melissa began rejecting normative behavior. She believed that no one cared about her anyway, so following the rules didn't matter. From her neighborhood friends Melissa learned to shoplift. Despite feeling shameful, she began stealing perfume, lipstick, and other small items from a local drugstore.

The things Melissa feared most were being alone and being put down or criticized. Her stealing was an act of rebellion, an attempt to feel important and respected by her peers.

On one occasion Melissa plotted to steal a beautiful gold watch from an elderly neighbor. She justified the idea because her own life was miserable. "After all," she reasoned, "Mrs. Hill is old and doesn't need that watch anyway." Melissa later realized that she victimized others in this way because she herself felt victimized.

To Melissa, the threat of going to jail for stealing was further confirmation of her aloneness. Her grandparents had warned Melissa that if she was caught stealing and was turned over to the authorities, she would be left to fend for herself. Melissa's behavior therefore mirrored the belief that "Others will abandon me. I therefore must meet my own needs."

Melissa began trying to escape her fear and pain by watching X-rated movies, drinking alcohol, and engaging in any behavior that would take her mind off her feelings. When she became an adult Melissa couldn't hold a job for more than a few months and was arrested several times for driving while intoxicated.

Faulty belief number three: "Life will never get better, and I am helpless to change it."

The deep-seated depression and learned helplessness that begin in shame-dominated childhood become even more significant in adolescence. Having gained only minimal emotional bonding with caregivers, adolescents believe that people cannot provide emotional nurturing.

During this important stage of discovering one's individuality, if adolescents don't trust that they will be safe or that others will provide adequate support they may adopt a frantic pace of activity to minimize their loneliness and boredom. They may make frequent and abrupt changes in interests, relationships, and hobbies. They may strive to satisfy a heightened need for excitement through thrill seeking, high-speed driving, vandalism, or conflicts with police. Such behavior is an unconscious attempt to satisfy the hunger for emotional closeness.

However, breaking rules and regulations further weakens these adolescents' bond with the community. Therefore, being caught only seems to reinforce the belief that "Life will never get better, and I am helpless to change it."

By believing they are alone and helpless, adolescents suffer intense internal anxiety. They have learned to anticipate rejection, so anytime someone stands them up, gives them a disapproving look, or even misspeaks, they interpret this as a personal affront. They tend to avoid direct eye contact with people, psychologically softening the blow of possible rejection. Harboring these foreboding fears, they constantly scan the environment for threatening remarks or looks. They are unable to relax or rest emotionally.

Tenet Two: Protective Actions

To hide from God, self, and others, adolescents with an Adam and Eve Complex develop a behavior pattern based on secrecy. Similar to Adam and Eve's hiding from God, shame-based adolescents want to hide so that others cannot discover who they really are. In fact, *they* do not even want to know who they really are!

One therapy client noted, "Self-discovery is uncomfortable. It's like finding out that you have warts when you didn't know you had them before." Assuming that what is inside is bad, ugly, and painful, adolescents avoid looking inward and try to prevent others, including God, from doing the same.

Just as porcupines hide beneath a shield of sharp quills, shame-based adolescents hide beneath a shield of secrecy. Speaking "false truths," they rarely reveal their true feelings. They share little and remain aloof in order to keep others at a distance.

Their own self-perception becomes further distorted because they listen to no one and have no mechanism by which to judge their own behavior. When they encounter criticism, they verbally retaliate in order to maintain false pride. No one must know of their tumultuous inner life.

To maintain this life of secrecy the shame-based adolescent may become a loner. Some loners spend countless hours staring at the television set, pumping music into their ears, occupying themselves with the family pet, viewing pornography, or getting high on various chemicals, including alcohol. Other loners hide out in groups of other youths. Usually incompatible with a group, the adolescent moves in and out quickly, unable to connect emotionally. When the group demands a commitment, the loner abruptly leaves.

Loner adolescents hide behind a different mask in every life setting and become so effective at changing masks that they lose sight of their real identity. This loss becomes even more significant as they move into adulthood.

Tenet Three: Deceptive Lifestyle

In adolescence a lifestyle based on deception, blame, lies, and anger grows into alienation and estrangement from God, self, and others.

Shame-based adolescents live in constant dread that their weaknesses and lies will be exposed, so they avoid or postpone making any decisions or commitments. They may employ fictitious claims to avoid rejection or to mask insecurities. For instance, whenever Trevor's mother asked him a question, he tailored his response to what she wanted to hear rather than what he knew to be true. Analyzing what others want and how to give them that information without risking self-disclosure becomes a major concern. Because they lack confidence in others' genuine good will, adolescents often offer any quick statement that might avert further probing.

Such adolescents are also emotionally discouraged, believing they can be neither loved nor accepted. Increasingly they blame the world—parents, teachers, classmates, and society—for personal shortcomings. They vacillate from being a victim helpless to change, to someone with no reason to follow rules, to being a person with the attitude that says, "I deserve special treatment from others."

They may express hostility toward their parents, even punishing them through academic failures, conflicts, and temper tantrums. Unconsciously they are saying, "Because you didn't love me the way I wanted you to, I'm going to be dependent on you and punish you forever." This spiteful attitude actually encourages self-rejection and further reinforces the Adam and Eve Complex.

Summary

During the turbulent physical and psychological changes of adolescence, the impaired Adam and Eve belief system of the shame-based child becomes even more pronounced. These unhealthy beliefs leave adolescents totally unprepared to cope with the onset of sexual development and the demands of a personal identity separate from their parents.

During this time the shame-based personality becomes even more entrenched. Just as Adam and Eve reacted to their shame by hiding and attempting to deceive God, adolescents also mask their true feelings. They become increasingly depressed and rebel, either through nonconformity or through isolation.

Adolescence is a training ground for adulthood. Behaviors during this period tend to set patterns that persist into adulthood. Such patterns, in turn, lead to a lifestyle. If the behavior patterns are deviant or antisocial, the resultant lifestyle will be deeply rooted in deception and estrangement.

Shame-based adolescents who are talented enough to succeed in sports, academics, or other activities have a much easier time with adolescence. However, their success mushrooms in adulthood, creating an ever-increasing standard that steers them on a collision course with their shame.

The way to lasting hope for adolescents with an Adam and Eve Complex comes through resolving the shame and restoring broken relationships with God, parents, siblings, friends, and themselves. The recovery process requires choices that may be painful. It also requires dependence on the grace of God. But when the process is complete, the results can be amazing.

Questions to Ask Myself

1. In what ways did I rebel during adolescence?

2. How did I learn about sexuality?

3. Which of my school experiences felt shameful?

4. How would I describe my relationships with adults during adolescence?

5. Did my friends reinforce Adam and Eve beliefs? How?

CHAPTER 4

ADULTHOOD AND SHAME

Lucy, a junior at a small liberal arts college, is one of six children. When she was small, her father labeled her an ugly child, and through the years he often reminded her of this deficiency. Lucy distinctly remembers being denied a new Easter dress. Her father remarked, "Why should I waste my money on a pretty dress for an ugly girl like you?" In addition, her father continually urged her to get an education because no man would ever marry her.

Beset by emotional pain, Lucy often speculated about whether she really was a member of this family or if somehow there had been a mix-up at the hospital. She felt so different from her parents and siblings that she began to wonder if she was even real.

To manage her feelings Lucy started to count things. She would count trivial things, such as the number of kernels of corn on her plate, the number of bubbles in her glass of milk, the number of ceiling tiles in her bedroom, or the number of hairs in someone's eyebrows. Counting was a way to remind herself that some things were real. Lucy's counting became a life-long habit and developed into the psychological disorder called obsessive-compulsive personality.

True to her father's prediction, Lucy never dated in high school. Today, in college, she still struggles with this issue. Her private logic tells her she is unlovable and worthless, so she lacks the courage to become interested in men—even though several classmates have asked her for a date.

Lucy feels so tainted by her life experience that she shudders at the thought of marriage and a family. Still, she does not want to be alone and lonely the rest of her life. She is terribly confused by her feelings and sees herself as out of step with the world around her.

Shame and Relationships

As adolescents move into young adulthood, a new set of challenges confront them: the life stages of courtship, marriage, and child rearing. People crippled by severe shame issues may be so alienated from others and so self-absorbed that they cannot even develop dating relationships, much less marriage partnerships. Terrified of being vulnerable with the opposite sex, they may isolate themselves.

Others become so skillful at hiding the core beliefs of their Adam and Eve Complex that they negotiate their way through marriage and even parenting. However, such people are often emotionally dependent. They may be exploitive, possessive, and jealous of their spouse. Because of their own self-worth conflicts and lack of supportive friendships they place high expectations on their spouse, demanding that the spouse meet all of their emotional needs. Shame-based people seem to emotionally fuse with their partner to make up for the deficiencies of childhood and adolescence.

Larry is one person who has done exactly that. Larry's Adam and Eve core beliefs left him victimized by low self-worth. He had little trust in his ability to earn a living and negotiate his way through life. To compensate for his perceived weaknesses, Larry married April, a strong, energetic woman who was charmed by Larry's need for care and nurturing.

Initially their life proceeded happily, but Larry's expectations of April only grew in intensity. As he became more and more dependent on her, Larry wanted April's life to revolve around him and his needs. He wanted to know where she was every minute of the day.

If she left the house for any reason—to go shopping, visit a relative or friend, attend a class—Larry would telephone endlessly, even having her paged at the grocery store. He could not bear to be out of contact with her. When April protested, Larry tried to restrict her comings and goings by shaming and manipulating her into believing that his behavior reflected his deep love. She should be just as devoted, he reasoned.

As time went on Larry began to view April as the sole source of his worth. He believed he could not live without her. April felt suffocated.

The Deceptive Lifestyle of a Shame-based Adult

Throughout childhood and adolescence, shame-based adults have incorporated the first two tenets of shame into their lifestyle. This lifestyle, maintained by a cover-up, manifests itself in blame, denial, and fault finding. Underneath the cover-up fester perfectionism, depression, anxiety, addiction, and abuse.

The consequences of this aspect of the Adam and Eve Complex are alienation and estrangement. Left unchecked these feelings lead to destructive or immoral behaviors that, in turn, reflect the third tenet of shame: a lifestyle based on deception, blaming, lies, and anger.

The Cover-up

The first thing Adam and Eve did after they ate the forbidden fruit was to sew together fig leaves in order to cover themselves. Shame-based individuals do the same thing psychologically—they create defense mechanisms to protect their vulnerable self-image. Blaming and fault finding are two common defenses used to avoid trusting God or other people.

The shame-based individual wants to be seen as someone who is self-sufficient, without weakness. That is why Adam told God, "The woman you put here with me—she gave me some fruit from the tree, and I ate it" (Genesis 3:12). Not only did Adam deny his responsibility for wrongdoing, he also suggested that God was to blame for having created Eve, and she was to blame for having offered him the fruit!

By focusing on others the shame-based person transfers responsibility to someone else, protecting the self and escaping all culpability. Evil and immoral behaviors are excused by disavowing responsibility and blaming others. This gives the individual permission to steal, commit adultery, lie, cheat, or violate others without feeling remorse or guilt.

Perfectionism

At age forty-five, Ted's life is out of control. He works unceasingly to make everyone and everything around him "perfect." He has been trying to do this since childhood, and now he teeters on the brink of disaster.

Ted's father worked for more than forty years as a maintenance man while Ted's mother stayed home to raise their three children. Ted longed for his father's attention, but his father was an extremely withdrawn man who would either watch television, tinker on junk cars, or pursue almost any activity that did not require interaction with the family. Ted, of course, felt abandoned by his father. He was also secretly embarrassed by his father's blue-collar status. Though not expected to do so, Ted went to college after high school, then chose a career in sales.

Much to his delight, Ted enjoyed great success in his career and became his employer's top salesperson. In order to achieve this, however, Ted worked sixty to eighty hours a week. Nevertheless, he was able to date occasionally and eventually married Angela, a sales representative in another division of his company. With their joint income they were making more money in one year than Ted's father did in ten.

Soon Ted began buying expensive new cars, jewelry, and furniture. Nothing was too expensive for him. For the first time in his life he was beginning to feel some sense of security. He could afford anything he wanted. He was moving closer to his goal—being in control of his life.

When Ted decided to build a new house he hired the city's premier architect and construction company and gave them detailed orders on exactly what he wanted. Relentlessly Ted pushed himself and everyone else in his life to make the house perfect. Before long he was arguing and fighting with everyone—his wife, the contractor, the workers, and even the bank. Nothing was ever "good enough."

Ted was so engulfed in the building project that he lost sight of his wife (who threatened divorce), his friends (whom he never had time for), and his faith. Unconsciously Ted was trying to prove to his father that he was worthwhile—that, in fact, he was better. In the end Ted's life collapsed amid emotional, spiritual, and financial bankruptcy.

Often a shame-based person such as Ted becomes perfectionistic out of a need to erase all evidence of any wrongfulness. Like Adam and Eve's fashioning of clothing to hide their nakedness, perfectionistic acts are shortsighted. They have only a narrow chance of succeeding. It seems unlikely that Adam and Eve truly believed that God would not notice their wrappings. Nonetheless, shame-based people always strive to hide defectiveness in any way possible.

Perfectionists are great performers. They believe they may be okay if they work hard, get good grades, keep the house and yard spotless, read the Bible and pray daily, are loved by everyone, or make a faultless presentation at work. The problem is that perfectionists have no internal reference point to judge what is "good enough."

Without an internal standard such measuring up depends on the criteria set by other people. Therefore, any negative reaction is an obvious sign of failure. Even a positive response from an observer can be discredited with "I should have done better." In either case, the perfectionist quickly reverts to the core beliefs of being worthless and unacceptable. The gnawing feeling of being deficient returns again and again.

Believing that mistakes must be avoided or, at the least, quickly covered up, perfectionists come to feel that no one truly can accept them. Like Adam and Eve, perfectionists believe that God cannot help someone who has committed a wrong, so they attempt to "clothe" themselves.

Despite what Adam and Eve believed, however, God had not rejected them. In fact, he provided animal skins for coverings. God understood that Adam and Eve needed something to insulate them from their shame, so he provided them with outer protection in the form of clothing. Later God offered inner protection to all of humanity through Christ's gift of grace.

Depression

By blaming their mistakes on someone else, people are saying that the cause of what goes wrong is external, that they have no control or power over their own actions. This view of external control is the underlying rationale for the Adam and Eve Complex belief that "life will never get better, and I am helpless to change it."

As long as shame-based individuals refuse to acknowledge their contribution to their problems, life will not get better. This reality begets an intense feeling of helplessness and powerlessness. Over and over shame-based people repeat in their minds, "I have no control over what happens to my life, so I must keep others off my back. I don't want them to see how bad or awful I really am." By blaming others they give away the very power they need to change their predicament.

That is what happened to Bob and Allison, who had been married for over twenty years. They were referred to me by their pastor for marriage counseling. Bob opened the first session by telling me that during their arguments Allison kept bringing up an extramarital affair he had had nearly twelve years before.

These arguments were rarely, if ever, resolved, so the couple typically spent days—even weeks—not talking to each other. Bob said that during these periods he spent most of his time "walking on eggshells."

Allison, meanwhile, told me that Bob's anger continually surprised her. It had surfaced again just a week earlier. According to her, she had found a passage in a book that described Bob accurately. The author had written that when men ignore their wives they are being abusive. "When I told him what the book said," Allison lamented with tears, "Bob got very defensive and blew up at me."

"Allison doesn't love me," Bob quickly shot back. "The only reason she stays married is because she thinks it's the Christian thing to do."

This couple was locked in a torturous cycle of blaming and fault finding that devastated them. Both felt depressed and constantly rejected by the other. Allison could not bring herself to trust or accept Bob since his affair. But she denied her rage because she labeled it un-Christian. Bob saw himself as a victim, unable to defend himself because his wife was more articulate and verbal. He withdrew into himself, silently blaming Allison for not forgiving him.

Neither Bob nor Allison saw that they were caught up in a fault-finding and blaming cycle. They each needed support from the other but couldn't come to terms with their distrust.

When shame-based people react to blame by retaliating, the target of their retaliation also begins to find fault. Thus, the shame-based person is deluged with yet more rejection. Over time the rejection, hurt, and loneliness, combined with the belief that "I am helpless, worthless, and unacceptable," beget depression.

In this cycle blame magnifies the alienation and loneliness. Bob and Allison's case illustrates this. Neither felt accepted by the other, so their marriage consisted of fending off each other's accusations in order to protect their own self-worth.

Anxiety

Another word for anxiety is fear. Shame-based individuals fear having their deficiencies revealed. To quiet this fear they attempt to control the people near them. They try to prevent anyone from discovering their real identity. However, neither life nor people truly are controllable, so the shame-based person must continually face rejection, mishaps, and disappointments.

For such people the unpredictableness of life creates severe emotional pain. They tend to be on edge. The body reacts to this pain by bracing itself to either fight or take flight; the heartbeat increases, the respiratory system strains, and the adrenaline level rises.

When sensing these physiological symptoms, shame-based individuals try either to overcontrol their feelings ("I should not be feeling this way") or to flee, psychologically or physically. In extreme cases they may develop agoraphobia (fear of open spaces), trying to leave the world behind by barricading themselves at home or avoiding cars, airplanes, people, elevators, or high places.

The shame-based agoraphobic mistakenly believes that

(1) external situations and events control their feelings; and (2) if they show their true feelings, no one will understand—or, worse yet, they probably will heap more shame on themselves.

By hiding these fears, shame-based people prevent others from accepting them. But unpredictability does not always mean danger. In fact, people often can be unpredictably thoughtful, friendly, or even loving.

Addictions

Today's society often has been called an addictive society. People are addicted not only to substances such as alcohol or drugs but increasingly to food, sex, gambling, work, or such activities as shopping, exercising, or reading. Any object, substance, or activity that has desirable qualities can potentially trigger compulsive, addictive behaviors.

In addictive cycles behaviors are repeated with such fervor that attempts at self-restraint are virtually impossible without some sort of outside intervention. Each attempt to stop the addictive behavior is overridden by an even stronger desire for the behavior. The addicted person is thus caught in a downward spiral of humiliation, discouragement, and powerlessness.

An addiction has an idolatrous quality because it is a substitute for an intimate relationship with God and for human fellowship and love. Just as Adam and Eve believed they could survive without God, addicted individuals believe they need only to depend on themselves and the addiction.

The alcoholic may say, "I'm okay as long as I can get to the liquor store." The compulsive gambler may say, "As long as I can come up with the right numbers in the next lottery..."

Looking to the addiction as a source of temporary relief for the longing and pain they feel, the addict holds these core beliefs:

1. I have worth and acceptance as long as I'm using drugs, feeling good from eating, making money, and so forth.

2. I can count on my addiction to meet my needs. It's more reliable than God or people. It's the most dependable source of good feelings I can have.

3. It doesn't matter if life gets worse as long as I have my addiction.

While an addiction may bring temporary relief from shame, each addictive act starts a cycle that fuels a sense of powerlessness and disgust and increases the shame. As the addicts' behaviors increasingly enslave them, the costs rise—divorce, health problems, auto accidents, loss of employment, bankruptcy, incarceration, or even death.

The gods of alcohol, cigarettes, food, sex, or money are neither forgiving nor nurturing. They only demand more time, money, health, and soul while returning less and less fulfillment and pleasure.

Abuse

Among the many types of abuse, the two principle forms are physical and sexual abuse. Sadly, the shame-based individual who was physically or sexually abused as a child has a strong tendency to engage in the same abusive behaviors.

Often such individuals harbor strong feelings of powerlessness as well as unresolved rage toward their abusive parents. Thus, when their own child acts in an "unacceptable manner," shame-based parents believe there is no choice but to mete out physical punishment, just as their parents likely did.

On an unconscious level such actions may release some rage, yet the abuse creates more shame because they have repeated the very actions that caused such terrible pain during their own youth! A compulsive cycle often develops, with shame and secrecy as the main ingredients.

Sexual abusers rarely understand their sexual actions, so each physical incident is followed by profound shame and extreme denial. An abuser neither takes responsibility for the abuse nor accepts the abusive nature of those actions.

Shame plays a central role in the lives of these individuals. They must blame and deceive others in order to claim that everything is under control. Sexual abusers use many self-protective defenses to avoid being discovered and honestly appraising themselves. Nothing is more terrifying to these individuals than entering a relationship that may require admitting their sexual behaviors. For this reason many abusers choose long prison sentences over treatment.

Both physical and sexual abusers find it critical to maintain the secrets surrounding their abusive behaviors. Their secrets allow them to hide from any responsibility for their actions.

While abusers may protest outwardly that others won't be able to live with the truth about these actions, in reality it is the abusers themselves who most fear living with vulnerabilities. Facing the truth would mean acknowledging shame and squarely addressing their own Adam and Eve belief system. If they are unwilling to do this abusers instead project blame, belittle family members, or coerce victims into keeping silent in order to protect the abusers' fragile self-image.

Through blame, coercion, and fault finding abusers transfer responsibility and deny the need to evaluate their behavior. All they need do is shift blame onto someone else. Once they find a scapegoat they conveniently accuse that person when anything goes wrong.

Tragically, the scapegoats are often the very victims the perpetrators have abused. "If he wouldn't have been so pushy, I might not have hit him," said one physically abusive father. One mother denounced her teenaged daughter by saying, "If you hadn't worn that sexy nightgown, your father wouldn't have come into your room." By directing the fault to someone else, and by refusing to take responsibility for their actions, shame-based people relinquish the power to change. In exchange their deficiencies persist unchallenged.

Alienation and Estrangement

Over time the lifestyle of shame-based individuals begin to exact a great toll. Unreleased, intense anger and rage become toxic. No poison is as strong as fermenting bitterness. Shame-based people virtually dry up like withered wood, and they are left with only one feeling: anger. They have forgotten what joy, love, and even sadness are like. Their range of feelings has seemingly disappeared, leaving in their wake alienation and estrangement.

Trying harder is one sign of alienation and estrangement. Already plagued by a deep sense of worthlessness, shame-based individuals strive to attain some ever-changing, ever-increasing external performance standard. This incessant striving for superiority is doomed. It only plunges them back into the core beliefs of the Adam and Eve Complex.

From a Christian perspective this lifestyle leads to estrangement from God because the individual, through personal effort, has rejected the gift of grace. The scriptures are clear: "For all have sinned and fall short of the glory of God, and are justified freely by his grace through the redemption that came by Christ Jesus" (Romans 3:23-24). It is grace, not self-striving or perfectionism, that atones for defectiveness.

Contempt is another sign of alienation. It creates distance between people and elevates one over another. The contemptuous person is perceived as judgmental, crass, or condescending. By showing contempt, shame-based people try to relieve their own inferiority at the expense of others.

This tactic, of course, doesn't exactly endear one to others, so the person feels put down or unacceptable. Few people, therefore, can get emotionally close to someone with an Adam and Eve Complex. Alienation and estrangement then create a self-fulfilling prophecy. Shame-based people become convinced that they really must be unlovable and unacceptable.

Evil: The Worst Consequence of Shame

Adam lay with his wife Eve, and she became pregnant and gave birth to Cain. She said, "With the help of the LORD I have brought forth a man." Later she gave birth to his brother Abel.

Now Abel kept flocks, and Cain worked the soil. In the course of time Cain brought some of the fruits of the soil as an offering to the LORD. But Abel brought fat portions from some of the firstborn of his flock. The LORD looked with favor on Abel and his offering, but on Cain and his offering he did not look with favor. So Cain was very angry, and his face was downcast.

Then the LORD said to Cain, "Why are you angry? Why is your face downcast? If you do what is right, will you not be

accepted? But if you do not do what is right, sin is crouch-
ing at your door; it desires to have you, but you must mas-
ter it."

Now Cain said to his brother Abel, "Let's go out to the
field." And while they were in the field, Cain attacked his
brother Abel and killed him.

Then the LORD said to Cain, "Where is your brother Abel?"

"I don't know," he replied. "Am I my brother's keeper?"
(Genesis 4:1-9)

When Cain realized that God had not accepted his sacrifice, the Bible says, "his face was downcast." I believe Cain's facial expression was an indication of shame. Cain likely viewed himself as deficient, bad, rejected by God. God, in love, spoke to Cain and confronted his shame by declaring that he needed merely to change his offering and God would accept it.

Clearly God was addressing the issue of shame; he was distinguishing between behaviors and personal acceptance. He even warned Cain of the consequences of shame—"sin is crouching at your door." Nonetheless, Cain's behavior progressed from a well-intended but unacceptable act (offering produce instead of an animal sacrifice to God) to an evil, premeditated act (killing Abel).

Cain's response to God's question ("Where is your brother Abel?") is part of the third tenet of shame. Cain's lifestyle was based on deception, blaming, lies, and anger. ("I don't know. Am I my brother's keeper?")

If we fail to deal with shame it leads to a breakdown in spiritual and human relationships, a life of alienation, estrangement, and evil behaviors.

However, the thought of exposing shame may be so threatening that people will choose immoral and evil behavior to cover up their shame. Psychiatrist M. Scott Peck comments:

The essential component of evil is not the absence of a
sense of sin or imperfection but the unwillingness to toler-
ate that sense. . . . We become evil by attempting to hide
from ourselves. The wickedness of the evil is not commit-

ted directly, but indirectly as a part of this cover-up process. Evil originates not in the absence of guilt but in the effort to escape it.[1]

Not wanting to face the alienation and pain, shame-based people learn to cover up their rage. They literally disown that rage-filled part of themselves by insisting that such feelings do not exist. They argue, "I don't get angry, not even a little upset. I'm simply not an angry person."

In order to make such a claim, however, they must expend tremendous amounts of psychological energy to rationalize and repress all awareness of such feelings. They use blame to ward off personal responsibility for their actions. To accept responsibility would be to reveal defectiveness.

In many cases these defenses may be so good that the person may even be a highly respected church leader, such as an elder, pastor, priest, or television preacher. Shame demands an intentional disguise and the willful denial of any wrongdoing.

Peck confirms this phenomenon:

Since the primary motive of the evil is disguise, one of the places evil people are most likely to be found is within the church. What better way to conceal one's evil from oneself, as well as from others, than to be a deacon or some other highly visible form of Christian within our culture?[2]

A good example of sin leading to evil behaviors is the biblical account of David, who looked upon and committed adultery with another man's wife. Then he attempted to conceal the sin and ultimately engineered the death of the woman's husband, Uriah. (See 2 Samuel 11-12.)

I believe David's sin of adultery was secondary to the evils of the disguise and willful cover-up of that initial sin. Sin is missing the mark or falling short of the standard that God has established; evil is hiding the sin and denying responsibility for our actions.

Summary

Profiles of the shame-based adult and the ensuing lifestyle patterns demonstrate that the unique and destructive lifestyle of the shame-based person arises from the Adam and Eve belief system. This lifestyle is maintained through a cover-up that keeps others from identifying the personal defects of the shame-based person. Unfortunately, this environment of secrets, blame, and fault finding does little to heal the shame-based individual.

As stated earlier, the consequences of the Adam and Eve Complex are a deep sense of alienation and estrangement from self, God, and others. Perfectionism, contempt, and bitterness validate one's Adam and Eve Complex beliefs.

The worst consequences of shame are the evil, immoral acts used to mask that shame. Shame-based people fail to realize that in order to reduce the pain they must stop the deception and blame and honestly admit their imperfect humanness. This clears the way for restoring their relationships with God, others, and self.

Questions to Ask Myself

1. How do I feel when I make a mistake? What happens to my self-worth?

2. What behaviors or pleasurable activities have taken on idolatrous proportions in my life?

3. In what ways do I feel alienated and estranged from God, myself, and others?

[1]M. Scott Peck, People of the Lie: The Hope for Healing Human Evil (New York: Simon and Schuster, 1983), 76.

[2]Ibid.

PART TWO

GROWTH THROUGH RECOVERY

CHAPTER 5

THE RECOVERY
PROCESS

Suffering: The Great Motivator

The church I attended as a youngster frequently offered time for members of the congregation to stand and "give a testimony." I remember feeling inadequate at those times. I could never overcome the sense that my life was not yet good enough. I cannot recall one person during all those years of testimony times who stood up and admitted that his or her life was a mess or out of control—for whatever reason. Apparently the only safe way to acknowledge mistakes or talk about one's pain or suffering was first to overcome it. Neither suffering nor focusing on its purpose was acceptable.

A common misconception today is that our shortcomings (alcoholism, psychological difficulties, relationship problems, family dysfunction) prevent us from ever measuring up to people we consider model Christians, those successful communicators of the faith we respect so much. By lauding them we label ourselves as imperfect and incapable. This attitude, however, perpetuates a lie.

The people most often used by God have struggled or are struggling with one or more major weaknesses. Often that weakness is the reason they have so much to share. However, our personal shortcomings are not the key but rather the capacity to accept God's grace and triumph over those shortcomings.

For example, Dr. Norman Vincent Peale admits that only because of his own fears, doubts, and tensions was he able to minister so effectively to others. A recent study of the lives of notable Christian leaders throughout the centuries reveals that most of them battled major weaknesses.[1]

I believe suffering offers a prime opportunity to confront our shame. Suffering pushes us to extremes, forcing us to examine basic beliefs about ourselves and God. The emotions that are an integral part of suffering—rage, anger, sadness, loneliness, fear—propel us to search for answers. Typically, complacent, unfeeling individuals are not likely to embark on a careful examination of their inner being. Thus, if we are feeling the pain of a shame-based lifestyle, there is tremendous hope!

Psychologist Milton Erickson believed strongly in the value of adversity. Crippled by polio as a young child, he spoke often to clients of the terrific advantage he had gained over others because of the total paralysis he had endured. Through his suffering Erickson learned how to overcome pain instead of retreating into self-pity. And so can we. Obstacles we cannot intellectualize away, con ourselves out of, or deny can goad us toward the promise of spiritual and psychological recovery.

Turmoil and Earthquakes

The first step in recovery is the realization, "I just can't stop this behavior, no matter how many times I try or how often I promise that this is the last time." Grief, loneliness, and pain become impossible to withstand. The rationalization, "I can do it on my own" has no effect. An overwhelming feeling of desperation cries out, "I'll do whatever it takes, pay what ever it costs, just so I don't have to feel this way anymore!"

Members of Alcoholics Anonymous use the term hitting bottom to describe how people feel when they have suffered so many losses that they cannot possibly sink any lower. The realization of having hit bottom typically motivates the alcoholic to seek help. Events that contribute to hitting bottom may include a jail sentence for a driving while intoxicated charge, loss of a job because of too many absences, or a divorce suit from a spouse who no longer can tolerate the alcoholism and all that comes with it.

Those who hit bottom never believed that their life could become so unmanageable, that they could slip so low. Unfortunately, some who enter and complete treatment later return to drinking and face another set of severe consequences. Will they hit bottom again?

When the Earth Begins to Move

For some people, hitting bottom does not adequately describe their out of control lives. Instead, they may feel as though they are standing at the epicenter of an earthquake. As the quake grows in intensity, the ground that supports them shakes violently. Nearby objects and buildings violently crash on top of them. The most solid rocks around them may become crushing boulders—being fired from a job, being hospitalized for depression or a suicide attempt; being kicked out of home, school, or church; being rejected by a best friend; getting arrested; or having a family member run away.

The tremor that precipitates an earthquake may be as simple as the innocent question of a small child: "Mommy, why are you always sad? You holler at me so much. I wish we could all be happy." An earthquake may look like the picture on the next page.

Besides the external earthquake, an internal earthquake occurs as well. This internal quake shakes our self-identity, causing it to slowly crumble. The picture we have of ourselves no longer fits reality. Our identity as a computer analyst, a church leader, a parent, a spouse, a boss, a homeowner, a softball player, a respected citizen, an usher, a hospital volunteer, a best friend, or a fun-loving person no longer seems true.

When the things we believe about ourselves cease to exist, a sense of alienation overwhelms us. We no longer know ourselves. We have no idea how to act or feel. The destruction of our identity creates intense fear.

In some cases an earthquake alone may not be enough motivation to change. We may need to experience worse consequences with even greater potential for destruction. The sight of our entire

world eroding before our eyes may finally cause us to realize, "If I don't do something, I'm not going to make it." This may provide the necessary motivation.

A man named Peter provides an example of an earthquake-motivated change.

Peter, married, the father of four sons, and a senior pastor for fifteen years, came to see me about his compulsive masturbation and the lust-filled thinking that accompanied it. Peter realized that he was slipping closer and closer to having an extramarital affair. An affair, if discovered, could severely threaten his marriage, his career, and his standing in the community.

The pain of crisis and the fear of life getting worse fueled Peter's motivation to change. Aware that the earth beneath his feet was about to open up, Peter knew he had to leap to new ground, retreat to the ground on which he had stood in the past, or stay where he was and hope against all odds that the earthquake would fail to swallow him.

Shame-based Christians commonly react to an earthquake by retreating to the familiar place of doing good works. They may read the Bible diligently and pray more, attend church with more frequency, and even shame other family members for not being spiritual enough. They are trying harder to be spiritual.

In my experience, trying harder to become more spiritual does not work. It represents an attempt to earn salvation and self-worth. As Jeff VanVonderen explains:

> *I now understand something about the nature and purpose of God's law—His standard—that I misunderstood for most of my life. One day the light came on. Our church was in the middle of a study of Galatians when I realized that God didn't give the Law so that we could "do good enough," and then pat ourselves on the back for being such good people. He gave the Law to convince us that we can't earn God's approval by human effort and to drive us to His gift.*[2]

VanVonderen solidly affirms the apostle Paul's claim that "a man is not justified by observing the law, but by faith in Jesus Christ. So we, too, have put our faith in Christ Jesus that we may be justified by faith in Christ and not by observing the law, because by observing the law no one will be justified" (Galatians 2:16).

When we are facing an earthquake, spiritual leaders often naively advise us to "pray about it." Such counsel, though sincere, fails to address the core beliefs of our Adam and Eve Complex. Consequently, we may feel more shame because we already believe that God must be rejecting us. We assume that if God had accepted us we would see real answers and real change. Our discouragement and shame increase as our unhealthy lifestyle persists.

Grace-full Renewal: The Recovery Plan

If we have identified the Adam and Eve Complex in our life, we may be asking "What do I do now?" That question is the focus of the remaining chapters in this book. The recovery plan that I call "grace-full renewal" begins by returning to the Adam and Eve Complex and undoing its principles, moving backward from Tenet Three to Tenet One.

First, grace-full renewal requires that we face the denial, deception, and blaming that have allowed us to justify our unhealthy lifestyles.

Second (it gets harder), grace-full renewal requires that we take a risk, that we face the pain by no longer hiding from God, others, and ourselves. Since we hide best from ourselves, we must start there.

Finally, grace-full renewal requires deep searching and meditation to recognize and face our faulty core beliefs. We must confront our sense of rejection that says, "I am worthless and unacceptable" and act and speak as if we possess great value. We must face our fear of abandonment that says, "I can only count on myself" and risk reaching out to others for our needs. We must come to terms with our deep discouragement and shame that says "Life will never get better" and replace it with personal accountability and responsibility by actively making decisions about our life.

Beginning Recovery: Facing Our Denial

When an earthquake shakes so violently that someone is forced to scramble for stable ground, recovery can begin. That is what happened to Diane as she took the important first step toward grace-full renewal.

An elementary school teacher, Diane is forty-eight years old. After twelve years of marriage, her husband Steve suddenly and unexpectedly filed for divorce. Four months later Diane came to see me because she had sunk into a deep, anguished depression.

As we worked in therapy Diane began feeling a sense of safety that helped her look inside herself for answers. During one session she revealed that she felt very distant and alienated from God. I explored her feelings in the following dialogue:

Levang: *Tell me more about the feelings of alienation from God you've had since your husband left.*

Diane: *I feel as if my life has been turned upside down, that I really don't know who I am anymore. I lost my role as a wife, as a step-mother. Many of my friends have sided with Steven, and I no longer see his family—with whom I was very close. I guess I don't know who I am anymore, and I blame God for letting this happen.*

Levang: *Do you blame God for your marriage not working?*

Diane: *I know it's not rational to blame God, but I feel as if he let me down.*

Levang: *Do you think, in any way, that you may be using blame as a defense? That by blaming God you may not have to face any responsibility for the break-up of your marriage?*

Diane: *I guess it's really self-pity—but I don't really know who I am anymore. I don't feel connected to God or myself.*

Levang: *Tell me who Diane is.*

Diane: *I'm intelligent, attractive, kind . . .* (Diane begins to cry.) *I'm sad because Steve doesn't want me.*

Levang: *I can see how very sad you feel when you are thinking about Steve.*

(Diane is now sobbing and nodding her head. After a while she admits she has been holding in her sadness for several days.)

Levang: *Diane, do you feel connected to yourself right now?*

Diane: *Yes, it feels better to let out the sadness.*

Levang: *How about God? Do you feel any more connected with God?*

Diane: *I guess I always thought God accepted me only when I was* *happy. My mom often used to say, "Don't be sad." I guess I've believed God couldn't accept me if I were sad.*

Levang: *I'd like you to consider God in a new way, by believing God can accept you, Diane, even when—and especially when—you are sad and hurting. God doesn't have to be a fair-weather God.*

Diane's story represents a typical response to suffering: loss of identity, feelings of disconnectedness with herself, blaming God for letting this happen, and a strong sense of alienation from herself, others, and God.

By changing her perceptions of God and of herself, Diane began to release those beliefs and attitudes that had long imprisoned her in an Adam and Eve Complex. Although Diane's life has not yet been fully restored to normalcy, this intervention proved to be the starting point for her recovery.

The road to recovery is a process, a journey. Beliefs and attitudes acquired over a lifetime are not easily discarded. In order to complete this journey successfully we must confront both psychological and spiritual beliefs, replacing what is not true with graceful renewal.

The account of one of Christ's most difficult experiences begins, "Then Jesus was led by the Spirit into the desert to be tempted by the devil" (Matthew 4:1). So, too, people begin the journey to recovery through an uncharted wilderness. Some, unable to make it, will turn back to their starting place with no change, no growth. Others will go through the wilderness of psychological and spiritual uncertainty, searching until they find the truth that changes them.

In order to go through our wilderness as Christ did we must come face to face with all of the arguments and rationale of our old faith system. We can expect to be tempted away from such a confrontation. Satan's taunts will likely exploit our Adam and Eve Complex, trying to affirm that we are worthless, stupid, and unlovable.

Our natural tendency when confronted with such shame will be to do as Adam did—seek others to blame. Blaming can distract us from our pain and provide a target at which to vent feelings. However, blaming does not work! Blaming is only a temporary cure.

An emotional earthquake may have destroyed our concept of

God, leaving us wondering if God even exists. That is okay for now. God can exist even if we don't believe in him.

In order to move beyond shame, beyond blame, we may have to say to ourselves, "All that I know to be true right now is that there is a God. I do not know if I trust God, if God's commandments are true, or if my beliefs about God are my own or my parents'." We can be sure that answers will come, but perhaps not immediately.

The spiritual and psychological journey I am referring to may explore four choices, but only the fourth leads to grace-full renewal. The four choices are:

1. Deny Conflict in Our Lifestyle and Become Disillusioned with God

By hiding from life and using denial or addictions we temporarily protect ourselves from the pain. We also begin to blame God for the terrible suffering with which we have been burdened. Subsequently we find ourselves disillusioned with God because we feel rejected by him. We feel angry that he has not stopped the anguish that overwhelms us.

2. Try Harder to Be a Better Christian

In this Adam and Eve response we try harder, doing our utmost to earn acceptance and love. This may mean trying to be the "best" Christian, parent, employee, parishioner, or friend in hopes that we can disguise our Adam and Eve core beliefs, preventing them from being discovered.

3. Continue Our Dysfunctional Lifestyle with Even Greater Fervor

Under the stress of our emotional earthquake we make a renewed commitment to our destructive behaviors. We desperately need to prove to ourselves that we are in control, because we are haunted by how helpless we feel to change our life for the better.

4. Discard Unhealthy Adam and Eve Complex Beliefs and Replace Them with Grace

The alternative response is to admit that we are suffering under the great weight of our out-of-control lifestyle and then embrace the healing offered through grace-full renewal. This means crying out for help. It means taking a risk, baring our weaknesses and pain to God and others. It means being honest about who we truly are—naked and in dire need of hope and peace.

My Own Earthquake

When I was twenty-two, I participated in an internship at a rural mental health clinic in western Minnesota to fulfill requirements for my psychology degree. After finishing my internship the clinical director of the agency wrote a summary of my progress.

In his report the director stated that he viewed me as depressed and in need of medication. In his opinion I showed little emotion and was unable to feel either joy or sorrow, ecstasy or agony. He also saw me as shy and inhibited in my ability to relate to others.

I wondered, Is this man really talking about me? He seemed to be describing a person void of feeling, numb to himself and the world he lived in. I had no idea, until that time, that I was depressed. And I certainly didn't know that others saw me this way. Yet after reading his report I immediately felt depressed—and terribly shamed.

As a Christian I had lived diligently by my understanding of Christ's teachings. I had created what I considered the most Christian environment possible. I had denied myself many experiences I considered unhealthy—dancing, movies, alcohol, sexual relationships—and yet this professional was telling me I was not okay! He was telling me my life was wrong, that I was abnormal. How could this be? I was as spiritual as I could be. How could I possibly work any harder?

The director's words were a serious indictment against everything I thought to be good and righteous. Despondent, I began questioning my faith, my God, my parents, and the values with which I had grown up. This was the first phase of my recovery: realizing that the rules, values, and beliefs under which I had been operating did not work.

This was my earthquake, a shaking that left in my path an enormous boulder I could not ignore. I had to deal with it. A war exploded inside me as my foundational understanding of life, God, and even myself no longer seemed valid. I had been living the best Christian life I knew how to live, yet I had no joy, and now I'd been labeled depressed.

The Second Step of Recovery: Facing Our Pain

Experiencing an emotional earthquake, even briefly, results in deep pain. From a physiological perspective pain is the body's way of warning that something is wrong.

In the scriptures we see God using pain to restore his people when they have disobeyed him, as in this example: "The people came to Moses and said, 'We sinned when we spoke against the LORD and against you. Pray that the LORD will take the snakes away from us.' So Moses prayed for the people. The LORD said to Moses, 'Make a snake and put it up on a pole; anyone who is bitten can look at it and live'" (Numbers 21:7-8).

Just as God asked the people to lift up to him that which was hurting them, he asks us to do the same. By admitting our pain we give others, including God, an opportunity to minister to us.

Anthony was just such a person who had to admit his pain. A self-employed electrician, Anthony came to me because he was suffering from anxiety. When he had come into a deeper faith almost seven years earlier, he had felt wonderful about developing a fuller relationship with Christ. He was enthusiastic about his newfound faith. However, in recent years Anthony had begun to feel increasingly guilty and shameful, distressed that he was not close to God. His self-worth had plummeted.

As an antidote Anthony joined a fundamentalist church that emphasized the importance of following all of the teachings in the Bible, especially reading the scriptures, praying, tithing, and attending church meetings. He tried to follow these teachings, but his busy work schedule sometimes interfered. He felt increased self-condemnation because of his inability to be the kind of Christian he thought he should be. His faith was souring like aged milk, yet he was immobilized by the fear that if he did not continue with his religious activities, he would be punished.

Anthony's dilemma is the second step of grace-full renewal: facing the pain. He had attempted to return to religious teachings but found that he still was unhappy and no closer to God. He also had mistakenly listened to his Adam and Eve core beliefs that accused him of being unacceptable. Anthony's internal talk so shamed him that, within the range of options or experiences Anthony had considered, he saw no way to make life different. So what did Anthony do?

This is the crucial step: choosing to look at the core beliefs of the Adam and Eve Complex—with the accompanying confusion, anger, and estrangement—and then changing. Changing may mean (1) denying our pain, (2) turning back to the old beliefs, family rules, and standards of the past and trying harder to make them work, or (3) returning to our former lifestyle and its behaviors. While we may perceive these alternatives as safer, they are not. Rather than helping, they are what has led to our present pain.

The only real hope-filled option is to forge into the pain, sadness, despair, and loneliness to face that part of our life that is not working. While this journey may seem unfamiliar and even scary, it may not be as risky as it appears. Many opportunities for change will arise in this honest search for meaning. Returning to what is familiar will likely lead only to a more turbulent life devoid of joy. So begins the recovery process at which I have been hinting!

The scriptures speak of recovery as renewal and transformation: "Do not conform any longer to the pattern of this world, but be transformed by the renewing of your mind" (Romans 12:2). Renewal is both a spiritual and an interpersonal process whereby we examine ourselves, perceiving life in new ways. Conducting an honest self-appraisal entails acknowledging our emotional pain and conceding that we have out-of-control habits, incongruent behaviors, estranged relationships with God and others, and that we do not even know ourselves. These elements characterize a pliable heart, a heart that is receptive to the transformation that Paul refers to in Romans.

This transformation is internal. As shame-based people, we must shed many layers of defenses in order to get to the core of truth about ourselves. We need pain and suffering to motivate us, or we never would take a leap of faith to develop a trust in God, others, and ourselves.

Summary

The motivation to recover from our shame-based life comes out of personal crises, times of suffering, and the great pain of an "earthquake." Such an emotional quake often savagely tears apart our external and internal world, resulting in overwhelming feelings of fear and apprehension.

Some people react by blaming God and denying their emotional pain or feelings of estrangement from God, others, or themselves. Some try harder to do good works. And others simply continue as they have been, even broadening their destructive lifestyle.

But in order to begin recovery we must recognize that our lifestyle has become unmanageable and needs transformation. We no longer can hide from the agonizing sadness and emotional pain brought by the Adam and Eve Complex. Instead we must want to seek the truth of who we are. This truth is hidden behind the many layers of protection that we have developed over the years to mask our feelings of abandonment, fear, anger, and distrust toward God, others, and ourselves.

Finally, grace-full renewal brings us to a time of deep searching and meditation that allows us to recognize and replace our faulty core beliefs.

Questions to Ask Myself

1. What has been my "earthquake"?

2. How have I avoided facing pain and suffering?

3. What areas in my life may need renewal?

4. What beliefs about my faith, life, and self may need reexamination?

[1]Catherine Marshall, "A Closer Walk," edited by Leonard E. LeSourd. (Old Tappan, N.J.: Chosen Books, 1986), 91.

[2]Jeff VanVonderen, *Tired of Trying to Measure Up* (Minneapolis: Bethany House, 1989), 90.

CHAPTER 6

PEELING THE ONION:
STRIPPING AWAY OUR LAYERS OF SELF-PROTECTION

During his early years Richard had enjoyed a very close, loving relationship with his mother and father. An only child, he had spent a great deal of time with his parents outdoors—fishing, camping, and biking in the summers and hiking and skiing in the winters. In Richard's mind, his had been a great childhood. But his adolescence was quite another story.

Just as Richard was about to enter the ninth grade, his father received a job offer in another part of the country. It sounded good—more responsibility, more pay, a step up. So the family moved. Unfortunately, Richard found the standards in his new community quite different from those back home.

In Richard's new school students customarily gathered after school to drink a few beers and smoke cigarettes before going home. Almost every weekend dances were followed by a long night of drinking and sexual activity. Richard felt very much out of place. He wasn't sure how to fit in and make friends. As a result his sense of self-worth began to suffer.

Feelings of doubt and uncertainty plagued Richard. Alienated and alone, he felt he had to join in. He became one of the crowd. His parents were, predictably, shocked and horrified by his new behavior.

Richard's rebelliousness lasted throughout high school, but when he began college he turned his life around. After finishing a four-year degree program Richard surprised his parents by deciding to enter medical school. He hoped that by becoming a physician he would atone for his adolescent years and regain his parents' favor and love.

As he progressed into adulthood Richard felt tremendous guilt and shame for his teenage years. His behavior had hurt his parents and he desperately wanted to earn their love and respect. Unfortunately, he focused so much energy on his parents that he neglected his own needs, never giving his wounded self-worth a chance to find healing. In therapy we were able to uncover his destructive motives.

Admitting Self-Protection

Richard: *I don't know why others won't take me seriously.*

Levang: *I noticed when you said that you were smiling. What feelings are you covering with your smile?*

(He pauses to think about this question.)

Richard: *I guess I don't like to show how much pain I have, so I've learned to cover my feelings by smiling.*

Levang: *Do you do this so others won't know how much you really hurt inside?*

Richard: *Yes, I don't want anyone to see my feelings.*

Levang: *How come?*

Richard: *Then they might know the real me.*

Levang: *And isn't that what you want? You initially said you want to be taken seriously. That means being known.*

Richard: (Pauses for several seconds.) *Well, I'm afraid. I'm afraid that if they knew me they'd reject me. They'd call me incompetent and worthless.*

Levang: *Can you think back, Richard, to who in your life you would most want to be taken seriously by?*

(His voice drops to barely a whisper.)

Richard: *My father.*

Levang: *And when your father did not take you seriously, what did you interpret that to mean about you as a person?*

Richard: (Tears form in the corners of Richard's eyes.) *I guess I considered myself to be unimportant, almost worthless.*

Even though Richard had become a successful physician and many people entrusted their lives to him, Richard's private logic insisted that he was deficient and unworthy. In therapy he began to grieve over the feelings of abandonment he had felt since adolescence and to consider his many unmet emotional needs. He also began to learn about his spiritual side, an important part of himself with which he had been totally out of touch. As Richard began to heal, his true identity slowly emerged.

The life of a shame-based person is very complex. Like Richard, we may function well in certain areas, yet sooner or later our pent-up emotions overtake us. Though recovery is possible, it is demanding and even exhausting at times. Still, if we focus on the task and complete the assignments found on the pages to follow we will be able to go forward, courageously facing our Adam and Eve beliefs.

Created without Shame

Here is the basis for our self-esteem: "So God created man in his own image, in the image of God he created him; male and female he created them. God blessed them . . . . God saw all that he had made, and it was very good" (Genesis 1:27-28, 31).

When God created Adam and Eve, shame did not exist. Adam and Eve were blessed and good. They were made in God's image by his hand. In declaring their goodness God put his validation stamp on Adam and Eve, giving them legitimacy and worth.

Adam and Eve's fall destroyed that legitimacy. Yet Christ's dying on the cross gloriously reinstated it. Our value and acceptance have been restored through Christ's gift of salvation.

God's declaration that we are made in his image means that he created people as truly marvelous beings. But when shame-based people live in conflict with the self they were created to be, tremendous difficulties arise. We become pretenders, actors, unauthentic people who cannot fully love because we lack a true identity to show others or God. Others cannot validate us if we deceive ourselves about who we really are.

When God says human beings are good, shame-based people do not believe these words. We see ourselves as deficient, so we do not believe that God can accept us as we are. As this disbelief persists, the relationship between us and God breaks down further. Alienation and estrangement result.

When shame-based people are out of control they may be depressed, addicted, obsessed, phobic, or abusive. Our lives may be littered with broken relationships. Physical pain may signal us that we are out of step with the wonderful self God made us to be. This is the earthquake.

It is also a time of celebration. The intense and overwhelming pain from a dysfunctional lifestyle may motivate us to begin peeling away the layers of self-deception—layers we have created in order to hide deep feelings of hurt and rejection.

The implications of John 8:32 are powerful for shame-based people: "Then you will know the truth, and the truth will set you free." Yet these concepts seem out of reach. Having developed a lifestyle of avoiding our true selves and deceiving others we may find it virtually impossible to develop deep, caring relationships. How, then, can we know the truth about ourselves?

Truths can be discovered in many ways—through experience, prayer, the scriptures, and the wisdom of other people. To deal with shame, however, we need to probe even deeper, to look carefully inside ourselves. In order to do this we need a new understanding of our emotional and physical selves.

Because God created us in his image we are an expression of truth. Yet often shame-based individuals do not trust themselves. We ignore the resources within. Through grace-full renewal, however, these vital resources will be brought to light. We will rediscover how our emotional and physical selves combined can be a valuable avenue for finding truth!

The Layers of an Onion

The road to recovery from shame includes a process of self-discovery, of finding our real selves again. The longer we have hidden our shame through self-deception, addictions, or an unhealthy lifestyle, the more self-protective defenses (denial, rationalization, and blame) we will have. These defenses must be shed like layers of an onion in order for us to expose the core—our true identity.

The outer layers of a shame-based individual's onion are denial, blame, and perfectionism. Beneath these layers hide the core beliefs of the Adam and Eve Complex. In order to address these core beliefs we must face many fears. We have to accept the sad fact that we do not know who we are. Then we need to realize that we must let go of a lifestyle that, although destructive, was at least familiar. These fears can challenge our desire for healing. What if I get healthy and others still won't accept the real me? we may wonder. What guarantees do I have that this will work?

This is a perfect time for another earthquake. We must make a choice to move to a new place now or suffer more fallout and losses. Earthquakes move us closer to grace as we realize our own inability to manage our life. Then we can acknowledge our needs and vulnerabilities. But only through grace can we recognize our imperfections and let go of shame.

Grace

Grace is God's way of eliminating our measuring stick of personal value. In both subtle and overt ways shame-based people have been taught that their value depends on behaviors. We come to believe that if we get good grades, have lots of friends and money, are popular, or have a good job, then we can say we have value and worth.

We often base our worth on an internal "value meter" that goes up when we do good things and down when we do bad things. Unfortunately, we often rig this meter so that accomplishments rate only a plus one or two while mistakes rate a minus fifty or one hundred. In this no-win situation failure can leave us feeling that we have no value whatsoever.

Scripture, of course, gives an entirely different perspective of personal value. We read, "In him we have redemption through his blood, the forgiveness of sins . . . "(Ephesians 1:7), and "therefore, since we have been justified through faith, we have peace with God through our LORD Jesus Christ" (Romans 5:1).

These verses do not say that we become worthy by our actions, success, wealth, or any other external means. Rather, our worth comes through the fact that God created us and Christ redeemed us.

By accepting that our worth is no lower or higher than others we gain a solid footing. We gain the courage to begin looking at the ways we miss the mark in all of our relationships. From this grace-full standpoint our value is a "done deal" and we can look at our behavior as mere actions rather than as evidence of our personal worth.

God's gift of grace is "good news," but the hardest thing for shame-based people to do is to receive a gift—especially one as wondrous as this. Gifts are totally counter to the shame-based person's basic core beliefs of unworthiness. Therefore, looking within ourselves to discover and replace our core Adam and Eve beliefs is both a spiritual and a psychological journey.

Two major psychological defenses—repression and denial—prevent shame-based individuals from uncovering their true self. These defenses, developed in childhood, have become a part of our private logic. We need to challenge them.

Repression and Denial

As children, shame-based individuals, like other people, desired to be loved by their parents, to be supported and nurtured by them. They also wanted their parents to be powerful enough to protect them from an unsafe world.

Because there are no perfect parents, however, this longing for love and protection often was not satisfied, particularly if neglect or abuse were common. Hence, we repressed feelings of rage, hurt, and loneliness because they simply hurt too much. We denied that it really mattered or even that we were hurt.

Yet just because we repress our feelings, longings, and desires does not mean they go away. Rather, they remain within us, rattling about to remind us of their presence.

These denied and repressed emotions demand us to respond to them. Because we did not respond at the time of the injury we are forced to try to control our feelings—possibly forever, unless we find a way to recover our true self.

Al and Diane Pesso, world-renowned psychotherapists, have developed a system called psychomotor therapy that provides a way to uncover repressed emotions. The Pessos have identified four steps necessary to discovering our true self.

First, we need to identify what we are feeling physically. Where is the energy in the body? Is the stomach tight? Does the chest feel heavy? Is there trembling?

Second, we need to know what that feeling or energy wants to do. What action does the body want to take? Does it want to cry, run, scream, or be angry?

Third, we need to identify the person to whom we are directing our feelings. Because people are social beings, they naturally want to direct their feelings toward someone, so this is an interactional step. Are those feelings toward a parent, a partner, a friend, or a boss?

Fourth, we need to understand what the energy means. This is the interplay between the mind and the body. What does the energy tell us about ourselves? For instance, if I have occasion to speak with someone who has treated me badly in the past and suddenly my throat and neck become so tight that I can't say a word, my body is signaling me that anger has choked off my feelings.

This four-step process worked for a fellow named Martin. When Martin was growing up his abusive father shamed and scolded him repeatedly whenever Martin would cry. His father insisted that only babies cry.

When his mother died in a car accident some years later, Martin dared not shed a tear, even though he desperately wanted to. He wanted to scream, "Don't leave me!"

The don't-cry rule and the great shame he had experienced when he was younger led him to repress his feelings. Part of Martin's self died along with his mother. From then on he would let no one get close to him. He no longer felt connected to himself or to others because his core Adam and Eve beliefs would not allow him to express who he really was.

In step one Martin discovered that his energy was a tightness in his chest. In step two this energy made him want to yell out, to tell someone how abandoned and alone he felt. In step three Martin found that his energy was directed at his mother. He wanted to interact with her and tell her how very angry and sad he felt that she had died and left him alone with his abusive father. In step four Martin understood his energy to mean that he had kept others at bay, believing that he could count on no one to meet his needs.

From this process Martin gained tremendous insight into his life and his inability to love. Yet insight alone is not enough. The shame-based person also needs to find the new possibilities and outcomes that God and life offer. Chapter seven will further describe this transformation.

Challenging Family Rules and Myths

When shame-based people repress and deny their emotions they severely inhibit their ability to recover. Dysfunctional family rules and myths contribute to the repression and denial.

Phyllis's life demonstrates how these dynamics work. Phyllis, a middle-aged woman, came to see me after her older sister disclosed that she had been sexually abused by their brother Robert during childhood. Some time after talking with her sister Phyllis's own memory was rekindled, and she painfully recalled that Robert had abused her as well. This memory led her to a path of self-discovery.

A soft-spoken woman, Phyllis always had been the "good girl" in the family. As a child she had listened fearfully to the sometimes violent battles between her older siblings and their father. Horrified by their behavior, Phyllis vowed to live her life differently, so she habitually repressed any feelings of anger. As time went on Phyllis grew unable to cry or show any emotion. As an adult Phyllis had few friends and was unable to get close to others.

Phyllis did not realize that since early childhood she had been denying her feelings. She especially did not want to believe that she had harbored any feelings of anger toward her brother. To do so would mean breaking her good-girl image. She also was afraid to confront Robert about the abuse. She expected him to laugh at her or refuse to discuss the matter.

Phyllis was afraid of anger—hers and others'. She had learned in her family that anger was bad and must be avoided. Her family's many unspoken rules, especially those about disloyalty, further quashed any expression of anger. To tell family secrets outside the family was to be a traitor, to betray those to whom one owed the most. Anyone who dared talk about the family fights or other problems would instantly be criticized and mocked. These family rules gave Phyllis good reason to deny her feelings and hide from the truth.

All of us have grown up under family rules, spoken or unspoken. Such rules, particularly those that are unspoken, are very powerful because they prevent family members from understanding the rules' intent. Often passed from generation to generation, these rules may have been useful at one point in the family's history, but they can be very destructive in a later generation. Only by discussing the family rules can we come to understand their purpose and decide if they support functional or dysfunctional behavior.

Family rules often grow out of myth and out of our mistaken Adam and Eve core beliefs. Myths obliterate the truth. The following are five specific myths we need to counteract.

1. The Disloyalty Myth: If You Express Negative Feelings about Childhood or Adult Experiences You Are Being Disloyal

Family rule: If you have nothing nice to say, don't say anything.

Truth: The reason a person talks about emotional pain is to get rid of it. Shame-based individuals want to be more loving toward themselves and others. We know that if we hold in our feelings, nothing changes. To be angry, hurt, or saddened by the actions of others and then to release such emotions shows how much we care.

2. The Emotional Responsibility Myth: Someone Must Be Responsible for the Family's Emotions.

Family rule: Certain family members must never have their feelings hurt.

Truth: Shame-based individuals are acting responsibly when they express their emotions honestly and respectfully. We are not responsible for how another person chooses to respond to us.

Since no one can reach inside other people's heads and control their thinking, each of us must be responsible for our own feelings.

3. The Peacemaker Myth: Each Family Must Assign a Peacemaker Role.

Family rule: The peacemaker must resolve all conflict.

Truth: Attempting to hold the family together at our own expense will only exhaust the shame-based person. This role prevents the family from experiencing the logical consequences that arise from unhealthy or deviant behavior. In truth this kind of peacemaking role does not resolve the family's conflicts. It merely serves to hide them.

4. The Heredity Myth: We All Are Going to Turn Out the Same.

Family rule: To express emotion is to risk acting like Mom (or Dad, or some other "offensive" person).

Truth: If we have read this far and honestly are attempting to change, we are different from the person we fear. We are not that person. We want to be free from shame. We should congratulate ourselves for our efforts to change!

5. The Going Crazy Myth: Having Feelings Drives People Crazy or Out of Control.

Family rule: Our family can't handle intense feelings.

Truth: Intense emotions can be scary. They may feel like grabbing a bare electrical wire. Yet with the caring support of others we can find safe ways to contain our rage or sadness. A therapy group, counselor, or understanding friend can help us accept and deal with our feelings.

By examining these myths and family rules we see more clearly the rationale underlying our repression and denial. Once able to understand the role these myths and rules have played in our behavior we can start to replace truth for this faulty system of thinking and acting. As we do this we will move closer and closer to discarding our Adam and Eve core beliefs.

Rejecting Shame and Blame

As shame-based people uncover and examine their family rules they will come face to face with their shame. Many painful memories may surface during this process, making us want to blame others for our unhappiness. Such feelings are as old as Adam and Eve.

When God asked Adam and Eve why they had eaten the forbidden fruit, they immediately argued that they were not to blame. No one, after all, likes to be at fault. However, Adam and Eve incorrectly believed that God saw them, rather than their behavior, as unacceptable. By failing to take ownership for their actions, they deceived themselves.

Bob and Allison made the same error. The more they focused on blaming each other for their troubled marriage, the more alienated and distant they became and the less they were able to accept their own responsibility.

After several weeks of therapy a major breakthrough occurred when Allison reported a change in her prayer life. She had stopped asking God to show Bob his imperfections. Instead she began asking God to open her eyes to her own shortcomings. Gradually Bob stopped blaming Allison and began showing her more loving behavior. Their relationship changed from one of fending off blame to looking for ways to show respect and love.

Shame and blame, whether in marriage or other relationships, can be aimed in any of three directions: given to others, received from others, or turned inward so that we shame or blame ourselves (a process called introjection).

First, shame-based people give shaming messages in many ways. Pigeonholing others or calling them useless places them in a category that precludes them from being unique, special, and, most important, themselves.

Criticism, of course, is another common way of shaming. Telling someone, "That shirt looks filthy. How could anyone be so stupid as to not know how to wash clothes?" shames the other by grossly pointing out the defect.

Nonverbally, sighing heavily or shaking the head can be very shaming. This is true especially after someone attempts to say something important. The unspoken message is that the person is lying or not worth listening to. This is rejection.

Belittling someone is also a form of shaming. Lecturing one's spouse on how to light the gas grill because "you foul everything up" or not allowing an eighteen-year-old to make his own dentist appointment because "you won't say it right" shames these people into believing they are incompetent and irresponsible.

Second, just as shame-based people give shaming messages, they also receive them. We can be shamed through labels, criticism, nonverbal cues, or belittlement. Anytime we begin to question our value or feel compelled to shy away from a relationship, we probably are being shamed. Shame-based individuals regard people in authority as a particular threat. Still, anyone who attacks or questions our adequacy may potentially shame us.

Third, shame-based people also can introject shame onto themselves through self-talk. Our inner dialogue throughout the day is highly susceptible to shaming messages. For instance, a man may call himself an idiot after nicking himself while shaving, or a woman may classify herself a failure because she lost her car keys. Although we probably would not accuse anyone else of being an idiot or a failure in the same circumstances, we are overly harsh on ourselves, regularly depreciating our own worth.

The more strongly shame-based people hold to Adam and Eve core beliefs, the greater the devastation wrought by shaming messages (whether given, received, or introjected). Consequently, they must construct a robust denial system to protect themselves from the assaults of shame. The good news is that as we begin to replace our core beliefs with grace-full renewal, shame will have less and less impact on us.

The more shame we feel, the more blaming and fault finding we will employ. These self-destructive behaviors need to be stopped, but first we must become aware of when we are giving and receiving shaming and blaming messages. We can begin by defining the terms.

Blaming is finding fault in order to avoid responsibility or looking bad. Blaming aims to deflect attention from ourselves in order to emphasize the weaknesses or shortcomings of others. Good blamers are so effective in finding fault that their friends and family become totally defenseless and readily give in to the attacks.

Shaming, on the other hand, is telling others that they are defective. Shaming messages punish others by going beyond finding fault to telling them how worthless, unlovable, and unacceptable they are. Shame-based individuals say these things to elevate their own worth.

Shaming and blaming may take place unconsciously. The act of communicating is very complex. It involves not only the shame-based person's words but also the tone, inflection, body language, context, and past actions. Many times we may not realize the extent to which our communication conveys blame or shame.

To better understand the messages we communicate, we need to observe how people respond to our messages. The following are lists of common responses to blaming and shaming messages.

Blame Responses

- changing the subject
- becoming quiet
- shutting down emotionally
- becoming angry
- getting defensive
- attacking physically
- attacking verbally
- crying
- leaving the room
- feeling like a child

Shame Responses

- looking downward
- having difficulty making decisions
- feeling confused
- engaging in self-deprecation
- apologizing profusely
- feeling powerless
- getting depressed

- becoming enraged
- feeling numb
- having one's mind go blank

Keeping Track of Shame

For at least the next week or two, keep track of the blaming and shaming statements you make and receive. As your list grows you may discover a pattern. Are there more blaming messages when you interact with your partner, children, parents, or siblings? Are certain friends more critical than others? Who puts you down most often? Awareness of such patterns will be helpful as we progress through the next chapters.

Self-shaming, in contrast, arises out of our own thinking processes. These are the messages we may be telling ourselves about how worthless and defective we are compared to others. To discover these messages, identify any painful or uncomfortable feelings and see what you are telling yourself about these feelings. If you feel sad and then see this as a sign of your worthlessness, you probably have shamed yourself.

To do this, create three shame tracking sheets like the ones on the following pages—one for giving shaming messages, one for receiving them, and a third for self-shaming messages. You may want to photocopy these for your own use.

SHAME TRACKING SHEET:
Giving

Date:_____

Event _____

_____

_____

_____

Person(s) involved: _____

_____

What shaming words, actions, or other communications did you
give? _____

_____

_____

_____

_____

Your tone of voice: _____

_____

Your facial expression:_____

_____

What message did you assume you were sending? _____

_____

_____

_____

What did you interpret this message to mean about your value, acceptance, or worth? _____

_____

_____

_____

_____

_____

_____

_____

Receiving

Date:_____

Event: _____

_____

_____

_____

_____

Person(s) involved: _____

_____

What shaming words, actions, or other communications did you receive? _____

_____

_____

_____

_____

Speaker's tone of voice: _____

_____

Speaker's facial expression: _____

_____

What message did you assume the speaker was sending? _____

_____

_____

_____

What did you interpret this message to mean about your value, acceptance, or worth? _____

_____

_____

_____

_____

_____

Self-Shaming

Date:_____

My shame-related feelings today were . . .

_____

_____

_____

_____

_____

_____

_____

_____

_____

_____

_____

The events or thoughts that triggered those feelings were . . .

_____

_____

_____

_____

_____

_____

_____

I interpreted that event or thought to mean that I am . . .

_____

_____

_____

_____

_____

_____

_____

_____

_____

Analyzing Shaming and Blaming

Charting your shaming messages may be a difficult task at first. If shaming and blaming have become an integral part of life it may be hard to catch yourself making these statements or hearing them from others. Have patience! By using the charts and increasing your awareness of what you say and think, you already have made great progress.

Seeing shaming messages in writing helps us to realize the things we have said to keep other people down while elevating ourselves. It also helps us to realize how blaming and shaming ourselves depreciates our self-worth. As our chart fills we will gain a brief glimpse of the devastating impact that shame and blame have had, and continue to have, on our life.

Summary

God created each of us in his own image, which means that even the shame-based individual was designed to know and live in truth. Adam and Eve's fall, however, created shame, which led to hiding and deception.

God's remedy for shame is Christ's death on the cross and his resurrection. Through Christ's actions the shame-based individual is given a gift of grace. This gift eradicates shame. Sadly, shame-based people feel unworthy of gifts and have great difficulty receiving grace.

By identifying our shame and releasing our repressed emotions we can look within ourselves for the resources that lead us back to a true relationship with God, others, and self. This process requires that we bring to light the ways in which we shame and blame ourselves and others. We must accept our weaknesses without condemnation.

CHAPTER 7

INTO THE WILDERNESS

In one of the most familiar stories of scripture, Moses leads the Israelites out of slavery and into the wilderness, where they wander for forty years until they are ready to enter the Promised Land. It is a story of human frailty and divine power.

During their wearisome journey the Israelites sometimes faced hunger, enemies, and other hardships. At first they seemed unequipped to handle the spiritual, physical, emotional, and inter-personal challenges of living in the Sinai Desert. Yet with God's help and the leadership of Moses, the Israelites survived. While God provided manna for them to eat and the Ten Commandments by which to live, Moses interceded for them and pointed them to the God who had delivered them.

The traveling must have seemed endless as they wandered for forty years. During their journey the Israelites questioned their leader, worshiped false gods, complained vigorously about every aspect of the journey, and broke every one of the Ten Commandments.

Only two of the adults who started the journey entered the Promised Land. However, neither God nor Moses (who died just before journey's end) gave up on the people. In time the Israelites crossed the Jordan River into the magnificent, lush oasis of Jericho.

Still, even after reaching the Promised Land, the Israelites had to fight for many years to claim the land as their own. Eventually they established a secure homeland.

Without entering the wilderness and facing its trials and tribulations the Israelites never would have learned how to be free people, how to function as a nation, and how to trust in God. Shame-based people, too, need to face wilderness trials before they can function freely with a firm trust in God.

Facing the Wilderness

Freedom from shame means trekking through a wilderness fraught with physical, emotional, spiritual, and interpersonal challenges. Just as the Israelites were unprepared for nomadic desert life, shame-based people may feel unprepared to deal with the struggles of Adam and Eve beliefs. In the wilderness we will have to search deep within ourselves, learning who we really are.

We also must call on God and others for support in the journey. This is vital to the recovery process. God said it was not good for Adam to be alone. People were made to be social beings.

In order to know ourselves we need others who will accept our imperfection and aid us in our quest. A skilled counselor, experienced pastor, valued friend, or committed support group member can supply the kind of assistance needed. Interaction with such people helps shame-based individuals learn to trust again. We discover more about ourselves as we see how our actions affect others. And as we learn to be vulnerable and discover that we are still accepted, our trust grows.

A Glimpse of Things to Come

While the Israelites were traveling to the Promised Land they learned new ways of thinking, acting, and living. They had to stop seeing themselves as slaves and begin viewing themselves as free people. In the same way, shame-based people need to let go of the old rules (the Adam and Eve Complex) and replace them with new core beliefs (true, rather than false, beliefs). We need to become grace-driven rather than shame-driven, changing our self-concept of worthlessness into a heart-felt belief that we truly are acceptable.

We must relinquish our feelings of abandonment and begin to trust. We need to stop acting helpless and begin empowering ourselves. Shame leads only to self-condemnation and despair; a wilderness experience provides an opportunity to overcome, to succeed.

The wilderness tests our beliefs and values while holding out much promise and hope. Freedom from our Adam and Eve Complex will allow us to find the love and peace God so generously offers. But to exchange false beliefs for true ones requires a serious self-assessment.

Moving through the Wilderness of Repression and Denial

In chapter six we learned that in order to really begin to feel again, shame-based individuals need to start peeling away at their onion. Some of the ways we can release our emotions are to: (1) identify our feelings (anger, fear, hostility), (2) give them an action to be fully expressed (yelling, hitting a pillow), (3) interact with others to express the feeling(s), and (4) attempt to understand the meaning of our energy and interaction.

Having exposed our feelings to the light, we can now work toward a new possibility—allowing grace in.

God knew that human beings were sinful and needed guidance in order to live according to his plan. That is why he offered us the wonderful gift of salvation. He sent his only son, Jesus Christ, to live among humanity and die on the cross so that we would be forgiven forever.

Grace is God's acceptance of us—despite our imperfections and sinfulness. Grace allows us the courage to be imperfect, to make mistakes, to be human—all without fear of his love being withdrawn. Because of grace we truly can give up our self-worth value meter and risk being ourselves in the presence of others. We can develop the exciting capacity to be the person God created us to be instead of having to hide from our uncomfortable feelings, our unacceptable actions, or our past.

Our new life, free from shame, depends on our ability to be ourselves—without all of our defenses. We can live without denial and self-protection only when we employ grace-driven core beliefs.

These beliefs give us license to truly love and accept ourselves. Yet first we must face those events that contributed to our Adam and Eve Complex.

Original Wounds

Having peeled away many of the surface layers of the onion, shame-based people soon get to the thicker layers—layers of sadness, resentment, and losses. These layers take us back to the many incidents in our past that hurt and damaged us.

The original injuries may have occurred in our childhood, but they grew in the fertile soil of our shame. Now, because they have contributed to our Adam and Eve Complex, we must confront them. Although these events happened a long time ago, we remember them now with nearly the same intensity of feeling as when they occurred. Our task is to work through the original wounds and release our pain.

Exercise

Take a moment now to bring to mind any memory or memories that have some emotional charge to them—memories that make you shudder, make your neck feel stiff, or make your stomach tighten. Write down at least one of these memories. Describe it fully, noting the situation, your approximate age at the time, the people involved (particularly the person who injured you), and your feelings. Write it all out as if you were a reporter on the scene. Don't worry about how much time this takes. It's important to describe the event in detail.

Next, ask someone you trust to listen as you read this recollection to them. The purpose of reading your story to someone else is that you need to have your feelings validated. You need to be told that these were harmful or painful events and that you did not deserve to be hurt. You need to hear that you're not crazy for feeling distressed and victimized by your memories.

The listener's role is not to fix or judge you but rather to witness that these feelings are true for you. Ask the listener to repeat back, word for word, each feeling you have described. Have the person say, "I can see how sad—or angry, or hurt (name the emotions)—you feel."

This exercise is important because we cannot confront denial until we accept the reality of our feelings.

After these feelings have been validated, the body may experience an energizing sensation from the feelings we have kept bottled up all these years. The body needs relief and resolution. We must set these feelings free. Some people find relief by crying, pounding their fists, kicking, or doing some other action aimed at the person who injured them.

It is best to satisfy this need symbolically. For example, using a pillow to symbolize Dad and his abusive or hurtful side, aim your feelings (perhaps by yelling) at that aspect of him. In this structured way, no one gets hurt physically; safety is preserved.

The next step is to develop a new way of thinking about the original wounds. We need to feel that there is hope, that there is a solution to the pain we have experienced.

To change the shaming messages that have become part of our core beliefs we need to create a new, "ideal," situation. That is, what would it have been like to have had ideal, completely gracefull people in your life rather than the individual who rejected and hurt you, causing you so much pain?

Remember how Mike's mother told him what a terrible boy he was? She said that if he didn't behave he would find her dead when he came home from school. He might imagine an ideal mother would say, "I think you're terrific, Mike. I would never threaten to kill myself. I love life, and I love you." Mike's ideal mother would have said and done everything he longed for.

Ask your support person to say to you, "If I had been your (name the relationship), I would have (name the actions)." Have this person repeat those loving words exactly as you want to hear them. It also may be helpful if the support person holds your hand, pats your back, or affirms the message in some other nonverbal, nonsexual way. As you listen feel free to ask the person to add any new words that come to your mind that would support and nurture you.

When you have heard all of the new messages you want to hear, take a few minutes to close your eyes and allow those messages to soak in. Feel the satisfaction, contentment, or peacefulness that comes from these new thoughts. Stow them away for later reference.

After completing the exercise, be sure to ask any support persons to repeat their own names, stating that they were role playing your ideal person. This is an important part of the exercise because it prevents you from becoming confused or later expecting them to be that ideal person.

You will likely feel tired, maybe even worn out after completing this exercise. This tiredness is a symptom of the heavy burden you have been carrying. Within a short time you will experience a sensation of lightness, a new sense of freedom. If you have more than one memory to work through you may find it helpful to do this exercise over a period of several days.

Seeing what a grace-full world is like can radically change your perspective. The wonderful thing about this exercise is that if we truly can imagine new feelings of love and acceptance, then our self-image will grow to allow more grace in.

Support persons play an important role in recovery. By acknowledging our pain and helping us experience the ideal they become agents of God, giving us the unique opportunity to symbolically witness what ideal love, support, and acceptance are like. And when we experience that kind of love we expand our own capacity to love.

Forgiveness: Letting Go of Shame

Forgiving Others

Janet is now in her fifties, but about twenty years ago her mother-in-law, Eunice, began criticizing Janet for failing to "raise her children right." Eunice wanted the children to attend the only correct church in her opinion—orthodox Catholic. Janet, a Protestant, felt deeply about her own religious beliefs and brought up the children according to her faith.

Janet saw Eunice's criticism as an indictment. In Janet's eyes Eunice had branded her a bad mother and a bad person. An insecure parent, Janet believed this assessment; it only confirmed what she herself feared. She wanted to push away her feelings of shame, but she found it easier to blame Eunice than to deal with her pain. Janet never summoned the courage to confront or forgive Eunice, so resentment continued to build over the years.

It is difficult for us to stop blaming those who have wounded us, especially when our pain still lingers. Some shame-based individuals erroneously think that when they "let the person off the hook" their pain and hurt will no longer count. Unfortunately, they only discount their own feelings in the process and do not allow themselves to grieve.

Other shame-based people may be too quick to forgive. They see forgiveness as the "right thing to do" and fear that God will punish them further if they don't forgive. Even if they can convince themselves to mouth the words "I forgive you," deep down the anger, betrayal, and distrust remains. Once again they have repressed their feelings, so they cannot truly forgive those who have harmed them.

By learning how to fully face the pain without telling ourselves that we are deficient and by sharing our wounds with others, we can let go of the onerous weight we carry. We can see the unfairness of life without seeing ourselves as helpless victims with no value. We can go through the process of forgiveness without feeling we should be perfect. We can ask God to show us how to let go of the injuries peacefully and grace-fully.

The hard truth is that for the most part shame-based people are responsible for their own successes and failures. This is one reason why the Adam and Eve Complex is so hard to relinquish. Ownership for our lives belongs to us. God will not make us stop resenting or blaming those who have injured us, yet he can teach us about forgiveness.

In order to stop blaming, the shame-based person must offer forgiveness. But forgiveness is a process and not something that can be turned on and off like a water faucet. Let's look at a concrete way in which we can move toward forgiveness.

Exercise

Think back to an individual who has hurt you, perhaps through his or her actions or words. What were the circumstances? What did you tell yourself? Where were you, and who was with you? What did you hear being said? Most important, what did you feel? What responsibility, justly or unjustly, did you take for the injury?

After thinking about these questions for a few minutes consider writing a letter to the person you have in mind. You won't mail this letter; it's primarily for your own resolution and healing.

In this letter clearly acknowledge your pain and the trauma you felt. Write about the lingering pain and how it affects you even now. Describe the situation without blaming, fault finding, or shaming.

Next, carefully consider how you feel about forgiving this person. What is true for you right now? Do you feel prepared—emotionally, spiritually, and mentally—to truly forgive this individual? Perhaps you need more time to consider this. Maybe you're not ready. Maybe you are ready but you're not sure how to do it. Whatever the case, add a line or two to your letter that describes where you stand on forgiving that person.

After you have finished the letter you may want to tuck it away and read it, say, in six months. Or you may decide to just burn it. The choice is yours.

The purpose of this exercise is to consider who in your life needs to be forgiven and how that can happen. Forgiveness cannot be taken lightly. It depends on fully examining the injury and making a conscious decision to let go of the feelings of resentment and bitterness. We need grace to do this. We need to replace our old Adam and Eve Complex beliefs with new grace-filled beliefs.

As we come to forgive those who have hurt us we will rid ourselves of old resentments and come to a new place of self-acceptance and honesty.

Forgiving Ourselves

Roger was quietly enjoying an evening alone with his wife. He had just returned from a lengthy business trip and was looking forward to some time with her. All of a sudden a loud crash jolted Roger out of his chair. His eye caught the silvery glint of metal. To his amazement, a motorcyclist had roared across the front yard and smashed into the porch.

Roger jumped up and called 911. Then he ran to help the young cyclist. The man was hurt. Blood rushed from his nose and a deep cut in his forehead. As Roger leaned over to pull the man clear of the motorcycle, he became enraged by the distinct smell of alcohol.

Roger felt fear, shock, and dismay. For the next several days Roger acted very irritable. Not quite knowing why he was so agitated, he came to see me.

In his early twenties Roger had been seriously addicted to alcohol. Like the man who crashed into his house, Roger also had had a terrible accident while drinking. As we talked, Roger discovered that some of his current feelings came from self-righteous anger. He couldn't understand how someone could jeopardize the lives of others and not care.

Roger wanted to push away these feelings because they revealed his own fear. He knew that the motorcyclist could have been him. Roger also discovered that he had not forgiven himself for his drinking or for all of the pain he had caused because of it.

Often it is more difficult for shame-based individuals to forgive themselves than others. Our shame gets in our way. Self-shaming messages tell us that we need to be punished for our wrongfulness. We do not want to admit to others what we have done.

Why We Have Trouble Forgiving Ourselves

Five justifications commonly prevent us from forgiving ourselves, but we can learn how to dispute them.

1. **Justification:** I can't forgive myself, because I deserve to be punished. Self-talk: I need to continually shame, punish, and heap guilt on myself, because I know I am deficient.

    Disputing statement: The more I punish myself, the more discouraged I will feel and the more likely I will be to make poor decisions. Knowing that I am capable, responsible, and forgiven gives me the courage to learn from my mistakes rather than giving up on myself.

2. **Justification:** I can't forgive myself or I will be forced to deal with my behavior and all of the havoc it has caused. Self-talk: I'm terrified of having to face the truth about my actions.

    Disputing statement: It is true that by forgiving myself and being accountable for my actions I will experience the full pain of my destructive behavior. However, there is a definite possibility that others will forgive me once they witness how much I regret what I have done. And the long-term consequences of running from my pain will only mount with time.

3. **Justification:** I can't forgive myself because I believe my lot in life is to be miserable. Self-talk: I don't want to get my hopes

up that I will be happy and life will change. I'm terrified that my life will be the same, and then I'll be even more miserable.

Disputing statement: Good things can happen to me, and happiness may not be so bad. Though it may be scary at first, in time I will come to appreciate the balance that good feelings bring to all of the intense, heavy emotions that I have felt for so long. Living a more genuine life means crawling out from under my misery.

4. **Justification:** I can't forgive myself, because it would mean that I am accountable for my actions. Self-talk: I want someone to blame for my unsatisfying life and all of my mistakes.

   Disputing statement: While it is true that by forgiving myself I will have to be more accountable for my actions, it also is true that by forgiving myself I will gain the courage to clean up the mess instead of staying in it.

5. **Justification:** I can't forgive myself, because my only security is in being helpless. Self-talk: I'm afraid to trust others; it's safer to trust only myself.

   Disputing statement: While it may be frightening to see myself as competent and on equal ground with others, telling myself that I have no value is inconsistent with God's teachings. With God's help and the encouragement of others, I can change.

As I said earlier, forgiveness is a process of slowly letting go and giving our struggles to God.

Exercise

Think back to one or even two incidents in which you have not forgiven yourself. On a sheet of paper fully describe this incident, indicating who was involved, where it took place, exactly what happened, and in what sequence. These details are vital because you need to know precisely what happened in order to consider granting yourself forgiveness.

When you have finished writing out this incident, sit in front of a mirror and say out loud to yourself, "(Name), I am considering forgiving you for (name the incident). Is there any reason you shouldn't be forgiven?"

Now answer that question out loud and see what rationalizations you use, if any. If you have none, go ahead and say to yourself, "(Name), I sincerely forgive you for (name the incident)."

If, however, you relied on one or more rationalizations you will need to dispute them, as demonstrated earlier. State your case out loud: why shouldn't you be forgiven? Take your time, being sure to list every possible reason. Once you have done this, say to yourself, "My worth is not based on my behaviors. I can accept and forgive myself and will receive God's forgiveness for (name the wrongful act)." Repeat this statement until you can feel the power of these words.

Your honesty has placed you in the position where forgiveness can occur, but it may take time. Be patient. Continue to ask for God's help, and return to this exercise as often as necessary. Repeat this exercise with other incidents for which you have not forgiven yourself.

Forgiveness brings accountability to shame-based people and frees them from their shame. It also allows us to stop condemning ourselves and others for our past. Forgiveness prepares us to exchange our faulty core beliefs for beautiful new grace-driven beliefs.

Summary

Venturing into the wilderness is a challenge for shame-based people, yet the experience will allow us to discover our true selves. In the wilderness our unmet needs and unresolved emotions—feelings we have avoided most of our lives—will be revealed. While we may want to turn our backs and retreat to the safety of our old ways of thinking, acting, and living, we must press forward.

As we address our original wounds and our inability to forgive ourselves and others, we open ourselves to God's gift of grace.

PART THREE

GRACE-FULL LIFESTYLES

CHAPTER 8

NEW ADAM AND EVE BELIEFS

"Remember that you were slaves in Egypt and the LORD your God redeemed you" (Deuteronomy 15:15).

No one knows for sure how far into the wilderness the Israelites traveled before they really could see themselves as free people. Some may have quickly believed they were free while others likely took a long time to accept this fact. However, as they began to act like free men and women, as they began to think as free individuals, they actually became free. And so can we.

Adam and Eve beliefs have kept us in bondage, with little hope that our lives could be better. Like the plagues that confronted the Israelites, our faulty beliefs have brought us disease—psychologically, spiritually, and physically. It is now time to break free from these destructive beliefs.

The apostle Paul writes,

Just as the result of one trespass was condemnation for all men, so also the result of one act of righteousness was justification that brings life for all men. For just as through the disobedience of the one man the many were made sinners, so also through the obedience of the one man the many will be made righteous. (Romans 5:18-19)

Adam and Eve core beliefs are fraught with faulty logic. God really does see us as valuable. Christ would not have made the ultimate sacrifice for humanity if he did not see great worth in us. Thus, it is time to exchange our shame-based Adam and Eve beliefs for beliefs driven by grace.

Confronting Shame

Faulty belief number one: "I am worthless and unacceptable to God, myself, and others."

New, grace-driven belief: "God has given me value and worth. I am acceptable."

Our fallenness and sin lead us to miss the mark in our relationship with God. However, sin does not make us worthless. The fact that God created us in his image and that Christ died on the cross for us proves our value. God wants us to worship and love him. If we were not important our feelings about God would not matter to him. However, the shame-based individual's feelings, needs, and dreams all matter to God.

As noted in chapter two, the belief that we are unlovable and worthless often dates back to our birth. Many infants come into the world unwanted, or their parents are incapable of providing the love these little ones need. Sometimes children are told that they were unplanned and were a burden.

This was true for Jim. When Jim came to me, he was experiencing a long-standing depression. Even though he was an extremely successful businessman, Jim had great difficulty seeing himself as an acceptable breadwinner, husband, and Christian. To compensate for his feelings of inadequacy Jim spent countless hours serving on church committees and studying the Bible. Yet no matter what he did he felt distant from God. He complained bitterly of how difficult it was to feel close to God.

Not surprisingly, Jim was distressed that he also felt very distant from his father. In one of our sessions we focused on how he had felt unwanted as a child. He was particularly angry because his father never had attempted to spend time with him and establish a relationship.

At church earlier that week Jim's pastor had focused on the scripture verse, "The Lord your God is with you, he is mighty to save. He will take great delight in you, he will quiet you with his love, he will rejoice over you with singing" (Zephaniah 3:17). The words from this scripture stuck with Jim throughout the week. He couldn't get them out of his mind. As he thought about this verse he realized that he did not feel that his parents, or even God, felt joy for him.

I challenged Jim to imagine God singing for joy when Jim was born. This was an unimaginable thought for him. He felt so unwanted, so unloved that even in his wildest dreams he couldn't believe that God would do such a thing. As an assignment I asked Jim to think about who in his life would be joyful that he was born.

When Jim came back the following week we talked over his assignment. Although Jim could not envision God singing for him, he could imagine his children, his wife, and a few other friends being happy. I asked Jim to imagine his actual birth with those who love him welcoming him into the world with singing and dancing. I said, "Imagine them saying, 'Welcome, Jim! We are tremendously glad that you have been born. We are excited to see you. We love you.'" Jim wept when he repeated those words out loud.

I then asked Jim to welcome himself into the world. This was more difficult. Yet after a while, with tears running down his face, he was able to say, "Welcome, Jim. I am glad you are here. You are a special child. Thanks for coming into the world."

I asked Jim to soak up these feelings and repeat the words until he truly believed them, until they became a part of the new Jim.

Later that year Jim had a birthday party. The invitation contained the following poem:

GOD DANCED

On the day I was born, God danced.
Did you really, God?
Was it a ritualistic, dignified,
bow-from-the-waist kind of dance?
Or was it just possibly a wild and crazy
arm-flinging kind of thing?
Did you pronounce somberly
that here was another 'good girl'
that you had created?

Or did you yell and holler and
grab the guy on the corner
to let him know that this time
you had really done it!
This time you created a winner—
This one was going to go all the way!

I hope you did, God—
I really hope you did.
    —Sarah Hall Maney[1]

To personalize the poem Jim inserted "boy" in the first stanza instead of the author's "girl." And to celebrate his birthday Jim hosted a square dance; he wanted to remember his birth in a new, momentous, joyous way.

God gave us life because he wanted us. He had a glorious plan for all of us who have experienced shame. "For he chose us in him before the creation of the world to be holy and blameless in his sight. In love he predestined us to be adopted as his sons through Jesus Christ, in accordance with his pleasure and will" (Ephesians 1:4-5).

It can be extremely powerful to explore the events surrounding our birth. This important time in our life allows us to get in touch with that small, vulnerable child within all of us. When we look back at these events with new eyes we can affirm our value. Let us do that now.

Exercise

First, engage your family or relatives in a conversation about your birth. Ask them if you were planned or a surprise, pleasant or otherwise. Were both parents present at your birth? Were there complications in your birth? Might you have had brothers or sisters with more severe problems that took your parents' attention away from you?

Second, look back at any baby pictures you might have, or ask to see those that other family members have. Do you look like a happy child? Who is in the pictures? What activities were taking place? Do the pictures show signs of love, apathy, distance, or tension? Can you tell who this child is and how the child is fitting into the world?

Next, place one of your baby pictures in a frame and put the verse Ephesians 1:4-5 on it, replacing the word us with your own name: "For he chose us before the creation of the world to be holy and blameless in his sight. In love, he predestined us to be adopted as God's son [daughter] through Jesus Christ."

Finally, place this picture in a prominent place—your dresser, nightstand, or somewhere you will see it often. Repeat the scripture out loud to yourself every day for the next thirty days.

Revisiting our birth, childhood, and adolescent years can help heal our deep wounds of abandonment and rejection. Since we cannot go back and relive our lives, we must give ourselves new healing messages like the one found in Ephesians. These new thoughts can become antidotes for our past hurts.

Faulty belief number two: "Others will abandon me. I must meet my own needs."

New, grace-driven belief: "God has not abandoned me. With Christ I can learn to trust others to meet my needs."

The primary concern of belief is the issue of trust. Shame-based people do not trust others to meet their needs. In fact, they lack the fundamental belief that there is anything in the universe that they can count on.

Karen's life demonstrates this lack of trust. Karen's mother was a diagnosed schizophrenic. Her father had strong feelings of inferiority. Very early Karen learned that her role in the family was to take care of her mother and her younger sisters. This situation made Karen terribly anxious. Her family's dependence on her forced her to be strong. As a young girl Karen's adultlike responsibilities convinced her that she could not trust others to meet her needs. After all, she had to be in control. She had to be self-reliant like an adult and not the child she was.

Karen's healing process progressed slowly. She had to struggle to give up her mother role. While it was destructive, it did give her life meaning. Yet all her life Karen secretly had hoped that one day the family would change and somehow she would receive the support and comfort she longed for. Karen realized that her role prevented the family from seeing her pain or knowing who she was.

In counseling Karen appeared very sad and hurt each time she talked about her childhood. As I shared that observation, little by little she began to gain an awareness of what life had been like for her.

At one point in our work Karen became involved in group therapy. After some time in the group, some of the other members told Karen that her lack of emotion kept them from knowing who she really was.

At first Karen got angry. "The reason I am so logical and unfeeling," she said, "is to keep my emotions from getting in the way." Moments after blurting this out Karen realized that she was minimizing her own feelings. Once again she was taking on the role of Mom, a person who took care of everyone else because she did not trust others to meet her needs.

The group continued to help Karen share more of her vulnerabilities. Meanwhile they kept assuring her that her role in the group was to be herself, not Mom. For Karen, being herself instead of playing a role was the starting point of recognizing that she would not be abandoned; others could be trusted with her needs.

Like Karen, all shame-based individuals must abandon belief number two because it hinders them from receiving support and love from others. Instead they must learn to accept the warm help that others offer and recognize their own worth.

There are many ways to ask for support. For example, Sally struggled with admitting her needs, but finally she was able to garner some help. The mother of three young children, Sally felt completely overwhelmed with tasks around the home. Her never-ending round of cooking, cleaning, ironing, and mowing the lawn, besides feeding and caring for the children, were more than she could handle. The work piled higher and higher.

Meanwhile Sally could barely muster the energy to get anything done. There was too much to do and no energy to do it. As time went on Sally grew anxious and nervous. She didn't know how she could get out from under all of the responsibility that weighed so heavily on her.

Sally wanted some help, but she was afraid of being rejected. Her husband was always too busy to lend a hand, and all of her friends, neighbors, and relatives had responsibilities of their own, she thought. Yet life was becoming uncontrollable and the demands on her were not going away.

While it was difficult to admit that she wasn't in control of her life, Sally decided to take a risk. She asked a good friend to come help her clean the house and balance her checkbook, things she had been putting off for several months. Much to Sally's surprise, her friend agreed. This seemingly small event became very important to Sally's healing process. She was finally able to overcome her distrust of others and ask for help.

In order to ask for support, shame-based people need to tell themselves that they will not die if their request is rejected. They will be the same person after they ask for help as they were before. There is no thermometer of worth.

Too often I hear, "It doesn't count if I have to ask for help." That statement belongs in the garbage! Any help counts—even if we have to ask for it! Often shame-based people expect others to read their minds. We are disappointed when others don't guess our needs and fulfill them. This continually locks us into a self-fulfilling prophecy of repeated rejection.

Shame-based people must tell others their needs. We must not discount the gifts of caring that we could receive if only we would ask. Instead we can thank others for their gifts. Actually, when we reinforce those who give us gifts we increase our chances of receiving even more from them.

Faulty belief number three: "Life will never get better, and I am helpless to change it."

New, grace-driven belief: "Grace empowers me to change my life for the better."

Belief number three leaves shame-based people feeling like victims because life is totally outside their control. They have no way to change it. Holding on to this belief leads to self-pity and self-depreciation. As victims we give up all control. We act and feel miserable.

Thus was Jeremy's situation. Jeremy strongly believed that he was helpless to change his unhealthy marriage. Consequently, he had been miserable for years. During one therapy session Jeremy reported that he finally had faced his worst fear—finding out whether or not his wife loved him. Arguing until two o'clock with her one morning, he realized that she really did not love or respect him. He had been afraid of this awful truth for a long time. After realizing her feelings Jeremy decided that what he needed to do was still respect himself.

In therapy Jeremy began to see how he had felt like a victim since the age of ten when his parents divorced. Assuming that his parents' divorce was his fault, Jeremy felt shameful about this. His Adam and Eve beliefs led him to remain a victim; he blamed his parents for his unhappy life and secretly demanded that his wife make up for his parents' shortcomings by loving him unconditionally.

As Jeremy began to face the truth, he saw that over time he had become an angry and stubborn man, taking his hostilities out on his wife and children. He decided that he was going to take control of his life. No longer would he allow others to decide whether he was lovable or not. For the first time Jeremy no longer felt in jeopardy of being rejected. He knew that he had confronted his worst fear and that life could only get better. He was not going to let others hurt him.

This was a new attitude for Jeremy. In the past when he got hurt, he put up higher walls to protect himself. Now instead of putting up walls, he was relying on the fact that he really was okay. His worth no longer depended on external sources.

Jeremy also recognized that it was important to really love himself and be true to himself—something he never had done. This change came slowly, but the realization in his heart that God did love him challenged Jeremy to discover his own lovable qualities, claiming them for himself.

Loving himself empowered Jeremy, and he began to share his true feelings with others. Expressing his vulnerabilities was no longer something he avoided at all cost. It actually became freeing to allow others to see him for what he was.

For the first time Jeremy began to know the meaning of self-respect. How wonderful it felt for others to see him without his heavy facades!

Once shame-based people are no longer in denial, they still have to face their worst fears—being unlovable, self-centered, worthless, or arrogant. Typically, the things that most upset us in others are the same traits we dislike about ourselves. By facing ourselves and allowing others to accurately confirm our identity, we will feel some pain. Now, however, we know that we are not unworthy human beings, we are worthy beings. This gives us the freedom to seek help. Perfection is not our goal; truth and love are.

The more clearly we see our true self—without denial, facades, and self-deception—the greater capacity we will have to change our life. The following exercise will help.

Exercise

Ask one or two trusted friends to tell you how they really see you. Ask them to point out at least two positive and two negative qualities. Write these statements out on paper to keep them clear in your mind.

Next, discuss what hidden resentments, unresolved abandonment feelings, or ulterior motives they think you might have, though you may not be aware of them. These elements fester beneath the negative qualities and actually help drive them. Stay open and do not try to defend your actions. Your worth is not in question!

Then ask these friends if they would be willing to help you change the negative qualities to more positive ones. Ask them to lovingly point out these negative qualities whenever they witness them, encouraging you to change. Also, ask them to affirm your efforts whenever they see you working to improve and grow in a more positive manner. You may want to rehearse these situations so that you will be sure to get the kind of feedback most helpful to you.

Finally, take some time in private to imagine yourself as a person with this new, more positive quality. Think about how it feels and how you see yourself. Consider how this change will improve your life and your interactions with others.

The truth is, you can change. Telling yourself daily that you can and will change empowers you to move forward and claim the life God has given you. God does have a wonderful plan for you, and with grace it will be yours.

Summary

To repair our core Adam and Eve beliefs we must replace our faulty logic, which says we are worthless, with God's promise of acceptance. God's intent for humanity has always been a glorious one. Abandonment can become trust when we allow ourselves to receive the gift of support. When we no longer see vulnerability as a sign of weakness we can tell others our needs. We can change our feelings of helplessness into feelings of empowerment by facing our fears and deciding to live an authentic life—even if it is painful at times. These changes in our Adam and Eve beliefs move us toward the unique person God made each of us to be.

Sarah Hall Maney, *Coloring Outside the Lines and Other Poems* (Excelsior, Minn.: self-published, 1982), 39.

CHAPTER 9

NO MORE HIDING

Something More
There is something more for me
something more out there
God is holding it in his hand for me
I can't see it   I can feel it
I know it's there something more

Sometimes it looks big
and powerful and prestigious
Something all the world will see
Sometimes, it looks small, insignificant,
unimportant to all but God and me

If I could wear it like a coat
it would fit me perfectly
going out where I go out   in where I go in

The coat I'm wearing now fits me, too
I like it   I'm happy wearing it
But my new coat will be bigger
than the one I'm wearing now
There will be room for something more

Is that what God is holding in his hand for me?
My new coat?
I'll need to grow more before it fits
it is so big
It is something more
*   — Sarah Hall Maney*[1]

At the time of their creation Adam and Eve knew they were so completely accepted by God that they didn't feel any shame. The Bible says, "The man and his wife were both naked, and they felt no shame" (Genesis 2:25). Though they were totally vulnerable before him in all ways, there was no hiding or blaming. Serenity reigned in the Garden of Eden.

Looking back we see how privileged Adam and Eve were. Love, trust, and peace were as plentiful as blades of grass. While their fall temporarily disturbed this wonderful existence, through Christ's redemption we are able once again to partake of God's goodness. The truth for shame-based Christians is that God's acceptance has been waiting for us all along.

Stripping away our self-deception to reach our core Adam and Eve beliefs has been excruciating. Still, this is a time to rejoice, because our journey has opened the door to a new self-identity. Though our journey is not over, we must celebrate!

Reaching our core has taken a long time. We have peeled away our many defenses. We have honestly faced the rage, sadness, and despair that nearly suffocated us. Ridding ourselves of this heavy burden, we have new found strength and courage. Grace has replaced our core Adam and Eve beliefs.

Grace, the Final Step in Our Recovery

Grace enables us to take the final step in our recovery—opening our souls to welcome God, others, and, most important, ourselves. Our life has changed irrevocably. We are acceptable before God, others, and ourselves.

We no longer need to cut off our feelings or deaden our souls. Happily, joyfully, wonderfully, we are accepted. We can be ourselves. We can set our spirit free. The emptiness that gnawed away at the center of our being can be satisfied. For the first time we will be able to allow love in, giving and receiving it freely.

Truly accepting ourselves gives us the courage to take risks, become even more vulnerable, attempt new skills, and follow our interests and desires. Failing is not terrible. We need not hide our mistakes or imperfections. Instead we can learn from them. Grace spreads a large safety net beneath us as we try until we succeed.

The new identity and new lifestyle that flow from self-acceptance move us to develop real intimacy, showing others our true self. The word intimacy comes from the Latin, meaning to make known. Genuine intimacy is literally making our true self known to others and allowing others to make themselves known to us.

Intimacy requires vulnerability, expressing our fears and wounds and believing that relationships are more important than money, sports, clean houses, success, and material possessions. Objects and actions wear out and hold our interest only for a short period of time. When we value God, others, and ourselves we experience a life that has solid meaning and purpose.

A New Way of Acting

The second tenet of shame: protective actions—hiding from God, self, and others.

Grace-full renewal: genuine actions—"I can be truly open and genuine with God, self, and others."

The result of having changed our core beliefs to new grace-driven beliefs is that we begin acting and living differently. This means we no longer hide from God, self, and others. Our life is committed to genuineness and acting out of this commitment.

Here are four grace principles to guide us as we work to act more genuinely:

1.   Examine our feelings, thoughts, and intentions.

2.   Share our vulnerabilities with others.

3. Remind ourself of our true value in Christ.

4. Freely give and accept grace and love.

These grace principles helped Jane turn away from her shame-based behaviors and begin acting genuinely. Shortly after her marriage to Andrew, Jane began complaining about her husband's behavior. According to Jane, Andrew never picked up after himself, didn't iron or wash clothes the way she did (which meant he didn't do it "right"), and couldn't even care for the family dog properly. Jane constantly belittled Andrew for the way he talked, the way he held his fork when eating, the way he packed his suitcase, and more.

Jane would become so frustrated with Andrew that she wouldn't speak to him for days. According to Jane, Andrew's "wrong" behaviors meant he didn't love her. If he did, he would do things right, not backward, she reasoned.

Though Andrew would protest and promise to try harder, it seemed that he never could measure up to Jane's standards. Unfortunately, their arguments grew more heated and Andrew and Jane began attacking each other through shaming, name calling, swearing, and threats of divorce. Their relationship took on less importance, all in the name of meeting the standards that Jane had set.

In order to recover, Jane had to look at how her standards were destroying her life. Utilizing the first spiritual principle Jane examined her own feelings and intentions.

The Bible teaches that "a man ought to examine himself before he eats of the bread and drinks of the cup" (1 Corinthians 11:28). When we hang on to personal offenses it hinders our communion with God and with others.

Looking back at her own life, Jane, who was the middle child in a large family, discovered that she had felt controlled and manipulated by her mother. Although Jane didn't experience significant conflict with her father, she and her mother had battled furiously over the way Jane dressed, how much makeup she used, how much homework she did, and the way she prepared meals and performed other tasks assigned to her. Jane believed that she never could meet the standards her mom continually set for her.

As an adult Jane feared criticism, and now she expected

Andrew to live by the same standards she did. When he disagreed, Jane's strong insecurities led to major arguments and hurtful feelings.

As Jane came to understand the dilemma she had created for herself, she followed another biblical admonition: "Confess your sins to each other and pray for each other so that you may be healed" (James 5:16). Jane admitted to Andrew what she was learning about herself. She cried as she recounted the many times she had been criticized, punished, and shamed as a child.

She did not try to shame or blame her husband for causing her unhappiness. Instead she sought strength from Colossians 1:22: "Now he has reconciled you by Christ's physical body through death to present you holy in his sight, without blemish and free from accusation."

After Jane could face her insecurities she began to realize that her old ways of thinking and old beliefs no longer were relevant. She stopped punishing herself and her husband for what she had lacked while growing up. She realized that her happiness did not depend on her behavior. No matter what happened, she was lovable.

As Jane began to accept herself more, it became easier to accept Andrew. He, in turn, responded differently. He began listening to her in a compassionate and supportive way.

In her daily actions Jane tried to apply Jesus's words—he called it his new command: "Love one another. As I have loved you, so you must love one another" (John 13:34). Jane stopped legislating standards—a form of conditional love—and tried to be more open with Andrew. She soon discovered that the more open she was, the less controlling and judgmental she was of his actions. Because of this change both Andrew and Jane felt more accepted and loved.

If we can courageously admit our wrongs, our imperfections, and our humanness, we can release the shackles of the Adam and Eve Complex. But this courage must be "rooted in the personal, total, and immediate certainty of divine forgiveness."[2] We must accept ourselves, knowing that we are not perfect, and then we can accept God's forgiveness. Only his forgiveness destroys the foundation of the Adam and Eve Complex.

A New, Loving Relationship with Ourselves

Having rid ourselves of the Adam and Eve Complex we can develop a loving relationship with ourselves. This means claiming our rightful place in God's world. Paul describes us as "children of God" (Romans 8:16). Then he says that "if anyone is in Christ, he is a new creation; the old has gone, the new has come!" (2 Corinthians 5:17).

When we accept God's grace we become new beings, part of his family. Gone is our defectiveness. With Christ we have great worth. Because our value comes from him, we no longer have to worry about measuring up. Peace can finally be ours.

We have now come to the place where we can and must look inside our hearts and learn to trust what we see there. Our Adam and Eve Complex prevented us from experiencing the full extent of our feelings, our pain, our sorrow. It blinded us to who we really were as people of God. It kept us from living a God-like life.

Self-acceptance is ours. We are lovable—unconditionally. Yes, we have faults and imperfections. Yes, we have value, gifts, and goodness. Yes, we are acceptable!

To look inside our hearts means to be true to ourselves, taking direction from where our heart (not our deceit) leads. Christ has given us value, and we need never fear being alone. We are our own friend. We must welcome this friendship, offering hospitality and understanding to ourselves. We must listen for the trust that lies deep within us.

As we come to know ourselves better we can discover our real talents and gifts. This information can help us make better decisions because we can see that some choices lead us away from our true identity.

Such was the case with Jeff, who at thirty-eight lives in a farming community near his parents and siblings. Hoping to marry someday and raise a family, Jeff came to me to work on relationship issues. But at this juncture Jeff felt little hope that his dreams would be realized. While he had had some success meeting women, commitment scared him.

The competition to succeed in Jeff's family was tremendous. Because they all had to "make something of their lives," each sibling tried to outdo the other. Also of great importance was staying in the community to carry out traditions. Outwardly Jeff accepted the rules, but life felt like a struggle and he often was depressed.

One of the things Jeff did during our work together was to take some vocational interest tests in order to better understand who he really was—beyond what the family prescribed. The test results indicated that Jeff was more interested in ideas and people-oriented tasks than the hands-on activity of his current occupation. According to the tests Jeff was very outgoing, yet his job required him to work alone. Jeff's natural abilities and interests were the opposite of what his profession demanded. In fact, his temperament was not even compatible with life in a small community.

Unfortunately, Jeff had been trying to fit into a mold unsuited to his basic personality, interests, and dreams. Because he was out of touch with his own feelings, he operated out of obligation and loyalty and slowly evolved into a person who was not his real self. No wonder he was depressed!

Over time Jeff was able to see himself more clearly. He realized that by forcing himself into a profession and lifestyle contrary to his heart's desires, he had stopped loving himself. How could he enter into a marriage and make a lifelong commitment when he did not know himself? It was impossible.

Jeff's story demonstrates how we can needlessly create unhappy situations for ourselves. When we force ourselves to be someone other than who God created us to be, our friendship with ourselves is severely jeopardized. And when we don't know who we are how can we make decisions about what would be best for us? As we learn who we are, we can capitalize on the gifts and talents God has given us. Then we can rely on our heart to know how to fulfill our lives.

A New, Loving Relationship with Others

Just as we need to learn to love ourselves, we also need to learn to love others. We can do this by creating an accepting and inviting space where we can welcome others without prejudice. This environment is built on acceptance rather than fault. Here we offer others our true self instead of trying to control or manipulate their thinking.

Our motivation is to know others fully, to experience their pain and joy, their successes and failures, their good and bad.

When others feel that our interest is genuine they can let down their defensive walls and begin to trust and love us. Jesus said, "By this all men will know that you are my disciples, if you love one another" (John 13:35). Only through our willingness to know others are we able to extend love to them.

Creating a loving, welcoming environment for others means not placing strings on our love. Conditions only foster insecurity. Forcing others to earn our love never works. They never know if our love will last.

God did not intend for us to exist in this world alone. He created us to live in communion with others, genuinely inviting others into our lives without demands or expectations. This is God's vision for all of humanity.

Reaching Out in Love to Those Who Shame

Our fear of being shamed has lessened. Still, it may be difficult for us to learn to love those who have shamed and continue to shame us. Thankfully, the once-powerful effects of shame have diminished. Shame no longer penetrates our self-worth as it once did. Nonetheless, while we are better equipped to handle shame, offering love to those who have hurt us is challenging.

How do we love those who shame us? Brenda and Jenny, two sisters, found this difficult but important. After Jenny and Brenda finished college, they decided to live together. They had enjoyed a good relationship growing up and thought that living together would help keep this relationship intact. They also could save money, an important issue because they both had large school loans to repay.

One day while her sister was upstairs napping, Brenda took the initiative to prepare dinner. Their parents were coming and Brenda wanted to use the time to get dinner started. When Jenny awoke and saw the work that Brenda had done, she was furious. Brenda was taken aback. Jenny should have been grateful for the help, she thought.

Jenny was upset because she had carefully planned the meal, selecting their parents' favorites. She accused Brenda of thinking she was incompetent and lazy. Jenny called her sister selfish and shamed her by saying Brenda was only trying to make up for past failures and look good in front of their parents. Brenda became defensive, trying to prove that Jenny was wrong by pointing out all of the ways she tried to make Jenny's life easier. Brenda left the house in tears.

Brenda and I explored the deep hurt she felt over her sister's behavior. Jenny's shaming left Brenda troubled, and she had not been able to think fast enough to disprove her sister's accusations. Consequently, Brenda felt alienated. She questioned Jenny's love for her.

When others shame us it is important to help them understand how destructive shame can be. We need to share how we have struggled with shame, telling them how difficult it becomes to regain self-acceptance. We must help them see that shame destroys. It cannot be tolerated. Shame is not of God!

But shame must be confronted with grace. As uncomfortable as this may be, we no longer can allow ourselves to become part of a shaming system. For Brenda, this meant telling Jenny how hurtful and untruthful her accusations were. Brenda had to be firm in asking Jenny not to shame her anymore, but she also had to learn to ignore her sister's shaming words. Brenda needed to remember that, regardless of her sister's statement, she has worth and she is acceptable.

When we stand firm in our convictions through the power of grace, then we can love others even when they hurt us. Our actions demonstrate that love cannot be earned; it is a gift.

A New, Loving Relationship with God

As we form a new self-identity, releasing ourselves of our Adam and Eve Complex, we will likely find our beliefs about God challenged. At times we may have felt that God was distant and aloof, too far away to support us. At other times we may have clearly felt his nurturing hand upon us. We knew that he was at our side, urging us forward. Still, at other times we may have blamed God for allowing bad things to happen to us.

Christianity teaches God's great capacity for forgiveness. It is now our turn to come to terms with any anger or disappointment we feel toward God and ask him back into our lives. The four grace principles are our guide in developing this new relationship with

God. We must examine our hearts and take stock of any blame or anger we have toward God. We need to express these feelings to him. We also need to remember that we have worth. It may be useful to pray for understanding and support in our emptiness. Then we must be open to receiving his grace.

Ending the Shame and Loving God

Remember Karen, who spent most of her life taking care of her family, so she didn't feel she could count on others? By neglecting her own self Karen turned to food as a way to satisfy her deep needs. As she continued to gain more and more weight, Karen developed an addiction to food. It was all she dared trust.

In the course of therapy Karen saw how she used food to hide her insecurities, especially her fear of letting others know her. Karen was angry at God for her overweight condition. She wanted him to help her control her eating.

Karen felt helpless. Her weight kept her from forming relationships, so she felt lonely and unhappy much of the time. Karen blamed God for not making her a more attractive and outgoing person, a person others would want to be with.

To move closer to loving God and forming a new relationship with him, Karen first had to stop blaming him. God was not the reason she overindulged—or the reason she feared intimacy. Karen's lifestyle was of her own making.

Without shaming anyone she had to take responsibility for her actions. It is important that we think about the feelings and thoughts that impair our relationship with God. Are we blaming him? Are we finding fault because we don't want to take responsibility?

Our hostilities and disappointment with God need to be brought into the light. God can handle this. When we purge ourselves of these bitter feelings we make room for God's love.

As with all friendships, an intimate and trusting relationship with God requires frequent communication and a commitment to honesty. And relationships take time to mature and develop. What is most important is that we start truthfully, admitting our doubts and questions. We cannot lie. We no longer can act as if we believe a biblical teaching if we lack conviction, nor can we pretend we have faith when we don't. We must stop hiding.

God will meet us precisely where we are, even if we are angry, disappointed, or disillusioned. God is all-powerful. He who created the world is powerful enough to accept us. We can pray as the man in Mark 9:24 did: "I do believe; help me overcome my unbelief!"

When we believe that God can accept us with our faults, questions, and wavering faith, then we can feel safe and our love for God can begin to grow. Our image of God then shifts from that of an adversary to that of a partner. As an ally God becomes a vital component in our continued healing. He removes our deep-seated feelings of abandonment by helping us realize that we are never alone, that we do have someone to turn to when we are in need.

The Process of Change

Letting go of our Adam and Eve Complex beliefs creates valuable new space at the core of our being. This space allows us to build new love for God, others, and ourselves. We have brought our pain into the light and have humbly asked others to support us.

The time has come for us to develop a new lifestyle based on emotional honesty. Purposefully hiding doesn't fit our emerging identity. The old is being made new.

By examining our hearts, expressing our vulnerabilities, acknowledging our worth, and receiving and giving grace, we can become fully human in the best sense of the word. The four grace principles foster a life of harmony with God, others, and ourselves.

If we really believe God is within us, then we need to search for truth in our suffering. It takes courage to share our anger and pain with God or with others. Still, if we want truth we must risk rejection. We must stop shaming. Then and only then can we listen for answers.

Summary

Adam and Eve tried to acquire knowledge by eating the forbidden fruit rather than searching for knowledge. In our past we, too, avoided the light because it showed our emptiness, our pain, our deceitful ways. Fully embracing a spiritual journey, however, lets us discover ourselves and, in the process, discover love.

Knowing our true intentions and honestly sharing them with

others help us become transparent, able to live true to God's plan. Paradoxically, truly knowing our own worth gives us less need to prove ourselves to others. Ultimately grace will help us let go of our self. Self-acceptance breeds freedom, and our once-fragile sense of worth gives way to a secure identity.

With deep trust in God we will resonate with profound joyfulness and satisfaction. Totally surrendering our self to him brings genuine communion and connectedness with God.

[1]Sarah Hall Maney, *Coloring Outside the Lines and Other Poems* (Excelsior, Minn.: self-published, 1982), 42.

[2]Paul Tillich, *The Courage to Be* (New Haven, Conn.: Yale University Press, 1971), 164.

CHAPTER 10

DEFEATING SHAME: A TRUTHFUL LIFESTYLE

A client once asked me, "Do I have to become naked in order to get support? It feels so humiliating to have to show my pain." To feel naked is to feel unprotected and exposed. Being this vulnerable is frightening. It may seem an extremely heavy price to pay for recovery. Still, the alternative only creates more heartache and despair. Pain is the body's plea for healing. And healing begins at that precise moment when we allow ourselves to express the fullness of our pain.

In our shame we falsely believed that our relationships didn't require us to be vulnerable. The thought of baring ourselves before others was horrifying. Yet now we know that shame distorted our thinking. We do not want to live superficially—alienated from ourselves and others.

Now we put our grace-full renewal to the test by presenting our real self to others. We apply our new insights and behave differently as we interact with those we love, those with whom we live and work.

Many of our friends and family members may be delighted with the changes we have made. They are proud that we have persisted in discovering the truth. They see that we have much more to give because we are presenting our real self instead of a false one. Nonetheless, everyone may not be pleased.

In many ways the changes we have undergone may subtly put pressure on others to change. Consider a situation in which the basis of a friendship has been to put down or criticize mutual friends. If we refuse to do this now, a conflict may arise. Our changes only make our friend's Adam and Eve Complex more evident.

The truth is that God designed us to need others. Our lives are interdependent, like a wind chime. Each chime is a separate entity, yet it is part of a whole. When one chime moves, it affects all of the other chimes, and they resound as well. While other people may not like the new sounds we make, we have committed to the truth. The old ways did not work.

To maintain our new identity we need specific skills and strategies to counteract shame effectively within our current relationships.

First, we need to assess these relationships to see them as they really are. Are they supportive, toxic, or neutral? If there is no love in our marriage or some other significant relationship, we need to face that. If our parents or children don't want us in their lives, we need to admit this. If friends never call us, we need to recognize that they may be disinterested in our friendship.

Sometimes, no matter how much love and concern we offer others, they still won't accept our love. We need to accept this truth and perhaps let go, grieving for what could not be.

But in order to stay in those relationships we want to maintain, we must find ways to preserve our self-esteem. Seeing our relationships for what they really are can be painful, but it is necessary for our healing. Now let's look at some specific shaming interactions and the skills we need to remain healthy.

Handling Criticism

When we criticize we are attempting to change someone's behavior. Because criticism implies a "wrong," it can generate strong feelings of shame. Usually criticism is unsolicited, and often it is given despite our objections. Hostile feelings typically accompany criticism, along with stern looks, shouting, and perhaps swearing. Often the intent is to hurt or punish rather than correct.

Criticism can be handled in a variety of ways. One of the best strategies is to remain calm by telling ourselves true statements. The truth is that we are worthwhile. Our value does not change simply because a partner, friend, boss, or someone else implies that we are unacceptable.

When we remind ourselves of our true worth, we can stop personalizing the criticism. It may be helpful to say out loud, "No matter what you say, I am still loved by God. I'm not going to allow myself to be shamed." By staying calm we buy ourselves some time to consider what the criticism was and whether the feedback was appropriate.

Rachel and Alex have had long-standing marital problems and are considering divorce. One of the ways Alex attempts to control Rachel is by intentionally destroying her self-worth. By so doing Alex believes that Rachel will not have the courage or strength to leave him.

To counteract his shaming messages Rachel has learned to say, "No matter how upset you are with me, I am still going to find a way to be happy today." Rachel took her sail out of Alex's wind. He had no one to fight with. Since she stopped getting upset, Alex had to discontinue his constant criticism.

Defending or justifying our behavior never works. The criticizer sees this as avoidance. A better technique is to admit our shortcomings without seeing ourselves as an awful person. Saying "Yes, I did make a mistake" allows us to take responsibility for our behavior. However, there is no need to put ourselves down. Simply acknowledging our humanity takes the sting out of making mistakes.

Still, if the criticism continues we may need to be assertive. We can ask, "Is your intention to point out my mistake or to punish me for it?" Retorts such as this usually prevent the criticism from going further.

Yet another technique is called "clarifying." This is one way to find out if the criticizer is intending to shame us or help us. When a husband comes home and says to his wife, "I can't believe you're going to that stupid meeting again," the wife can respond this way: "Tell me, dear, just what is it that you don't like about my going to this meeting?" Or, "How is this meeting a problem for you?"

By asking criticizers to point out exactly what part of our behavior bothers them, we place the problem with them and not ourselves. This forces critics to deal with the problem in a more adult manner.

Manipulation

People who manipulate are trying to control or influence us in order to get their own way. Instead of telling us what they want, they try to shame or trick us into giving them something. Manipulators hinder us from giving freely because they don't directly ask for anything. Instead they subtly imply that we are terrible or disrespectful if we don't give in to their pressure. Rarely does anyone feel good about giving to a manipulator, because force dethrones free choice.

Tom's mother, Alice, broke her leg in a fall and was transferred to a nursing home to ensure adequate care. Though Alice badly wanted to return home, she resisted all attempts by the nursing staff to help her regain her ability to function independently.

But Alice is a master at manipulation. During a conference to assess her progress Alice blamed Tom for all of her troubles and said that if she didn't return home, she would die. She intended to shame Tom into having her released.

Though Tom felt distressed by his mother's shaming statements, he told her how painful it was to see her unwilling to do anything for herself. He would not allow himself to be controlled. If she wanted to go home, then she would have to take responsibility for making this happen.

By stating what was true and clarifying his mother's responsibilities, Tom refused to be manipulated. And when Alice saw that her attempt to trick Tom did not work, she backed down. By bringing honesty to their relationship Alice and Tom finally could address the deeper issue—Alice's fear of dying, a subject that Alice had avoided talking about.

Fear of Hurting Others

All of the hurts we have suffered have made us more tender-hearted. We are distressed when we see others in pain. This tender-heartedness can be a problem if we allow ourselves to be shamed while protecting the feelings of others. This happens when we say, "I can't possibly tell them how I really feel because it would hurt them" or "I don't want to make an issue of this, for they might get hurt." In the process of protecting others, we jeopardize our recovery. We risk returning to our Adam and Eve core beliefs.

This was the danger Sean faced. At age twelve Sean had been sexually abused by his minister. Although the abuse lasted nearly a year, Sean never told his family. He was afraid that telling the truth would hurt everyone—his parents, the rest of the family, and the pastor. Sean felt so alone that at age fifteen he attempted to commit suicide.

As an adult Sean now understands how harmful it is to protect others from the truth because they might get hurt. It almost cost him his life. Certainly we will be tactful and caring when we confront those who shame us. But to hold in and deny shame's damage endangers our recovery.

Developing New Relationships

In addition to learning how to deal more responsibly with our current relationships, many of us may want to develop new relationships, too. Ironically, the better friend we are to ourselves, the more friends we likely will have. We already have made great progress by coming to know and accept ourselves. Now we can form close relationships with others more easily.

Because we were stuck in the rut of our Adam and Eve Complex, we may have stopped pursuing hobbies or activities that captivated our interests. Now is the time to rediscover that hobby or learn something new, like taking a class in gardening, joining an exercise program, or dusting off that saxophone and taking music lessons.

As the joys of life begin to fill our heart we likely will feel freer, more alive. It feels good to actively pursue life. As an extra payoff, our new pursuits may generate more opportunities to meet people of similar interests.

Often our Adam and Eve Complex has crippled our social skills. Relating to others can be difficult. We may have trouble making eye contact. Smiling or engaging others in conversation may not come easy. Much of this results from our past inability to accept ourselves as worthwhile human beings.

Many people find it helpful to practice these underused skills. Make a genuine effort to look directly at others at least once each day. Smile often. Strike up a conversation with a stranger at least once a week. These things strengthen our interpersonal skills. We may be surprised how positively others will respond to us when we make a concerted effort to be open and personable.

For those who are shy it is particularly important to overcome feelings of inadequacy. Often shy people fear that they may say something "dumb" or "stupid." They mistakenly believe that they are totally responsible for keeping the conversation going. Silences produce terror.

Yet the truth is that conversations are a shared responsibility. A conversation is best thought of as a mutual opportunity to genuinely get to know someone rather than a test of our intelligence or wit. When we think in these terms, conversations can become pleasant, even exciting.

If we reflect a genuine concern for others, it likely will be reciprocated. And when there is mutual respect, lulls in the conversation can be restful.

A Truthful Lifestyle

The third tenet of shame: deceptive lifestyle—A lifestyle based on self-deception, lies, and anger that leaves the individual alienated and estranged from God, self, and others.

Grace-full renewal: truthful lifestyle—"A lifestyle based on honesty, respect, forgiveness, and nurturance that brings me into communion with God, self, and others."

As we struggle to defeat and counteract the shame around us we see that recovery is an ongoing process. These continual challenges demand a solid footing from which to battle adversity. Our new lifestyle must be one based on truth rather than deceit.

How do we maintain the new lifestyle we have worked so hard to develop? Once again, four qualities that promote a truthful lifestyle are: honesty, respect, forgiveness, and nurturance.

Honesty

When we let go of our shame-based identity and reclaim our true value through Christ, we no longer want to pretend, to lie, to deceive. We see our relationships for what they are—some nurturing, some destructive, some pointless. We cannot tolerate superficiality. Sharing with others our vulnerabilities, our dreams, our fears, our hurts, our self has become more natural. We truly want to be known and to know others.

Our commitment to honesty does not mean that we are always involved in deep conversations, sharing our very souls. We can laugh when we want to and talk seriously when we need to. We no longer are locked into our family role of clown, scapegoat, or pleaser. We can be ourselves.

Here are some practical action steps you can take to promote honesty:

1. Ask others not to keep secrets. The power of secrets is not in the information itself but in withholding information. Keeping secrets only handcuffs us from the truth and perpetuates the myth that the truth is so awful that no one can handle it. We must reassure others that we can handle the truth, even if it hurts.

2. Build or develop the type of loving relationship wherein positive and negative feelings can be expressed. It is important to know where we stand with others. We need to hear when we have disappointed them or let them down. We also need to hear what they like or admire about us.

3. Stop telling "little white lies." Though they may seem harmless, little white lies are a form of emotional dishonesty. They make us look good or help us avoid responsibility. Yet more than anything they create distance in our relationships. When asked how we're doing we don't have to give the standard reply, pretending we're fine when we're not. We can say what is true.

Respect

The word respect is often misused. For some, respect means not questioning those in authority. Others see respect as saying only proper things or repeating only what we think others want us to say. However, healthy respect means treating others with honor and worth. Respect means believing in others, encouraging others, and looking for the good in others. Respect also can mean actually listening to what others say and treating them like capable individuals.

To ensure that we are respected and that we respect others we can take the following actions:

1. Let others know how we want to be treated. If we wish to be called before others visit us, tell them. If we want to be addressed by our proper name, let them know this. People cannot read our minds. We must tell them what we want.

2. Model respect for others by following Christ's commandment to love others as ourselves. If Christ lived next door to us, what kind of neighbor would he be? What actions would demonstrate how considerate, generous, and thoughtful he is? By putting ourselves in Christ's sandals we will find it easier to love others—and in the process love ourselves.

Forgiveness

Those we let closest to our heart have the greatest capacity to love and nurture us. But they also have the greatest capacity to injure us. We need great courage and a strong foundation of grace to forgive those who have been cruel or hurtful to us. The alternative is to hold in the anger, bitterness, and rage, but these things only impair our healing.

Forgiveness needs to become a way of life. Everyone makes mistakes. Therefore, continual forgiveness is essential to healthy relationships. We continually need to relearn how to accept and give forgiveness.

The following are a few action steps to help us develop our ability to forgive:

1. Create a "burden basket." Write down the names and incidents of those individuals we have not been able to forgive. Place the list in a basket or similar container, giving the resentment and bitterness over to God.

2. Turn a hurt around through an act of kindness. When we are hurt, our first reaction might be to strike back. Yet that resolves nothing. To react differently, we can admit that we are hurt and then find a way to reach out to someone else in need. Volunteering at church, a nursing home, or a hospital can give us a new perspective on our pain and help us let go of the resentment we may be feeling.

3. Pray that we can accept those we have had difficulty forgiving. Sometimes in our heart we truly want to forgive certain people, yet whenever we think of them, our neck gets tight and our stomach churns. We can ask God for help in learning how to fully forgive them. It may not happen immediately; however, we can be sure that it will happen. We can learn how to forgive.

Nurturance

In the throes of our Adam and Eve Complex we would not allow others to nurture us. Intimacy frightened and confused us. But as we truly accept our inherent worth, we can readily receive the nurturing others offer and we can learn how to reciprocate.

Nurturing can be expressed through touch, words, attitudes, and actions.

One of the most powerful ways we are nurtured is by touch. Our bodies are made up of more than a half million sensory fibers, making our skin the most powerful sensory organ. Studies have shown that babies can become hyperactive, irritable, and depressed, and even can die without touch.

We all need to be touched, yet many of us avoid it because we associate touch with sexual emotions. In particular, if we have been sexually abused our bodies often confuse healthy touch with past abuse. Still, we all must learn to give and receive touch in a nonsexual way. A warm embrace, a comforting pat on the shoulder, a squeeze of the hand all relay the message of care and love.

Nurturing also is expressed through words, attitudes, and actions. Being sensitive to and anticipating the needs of others is a form of nurturing. We can do this by providing a word of encouragement to a friend after a trying day or making a point not to miss our child's school activities. Likewise, we are nurtured when friends drop by unexpectedly to take us to breakfast or siblings call to see if there is any way they can be of help.

We may know what nurturance is, but we may not have experienced much of it. For now we can take small steps and learn as we go. The way others nurture us can become our model in nurturing others.

The following action steps are a way to begin giving and receiving nurturance.

1.   When saying good-bye, consider giving a hug instead of a handshake. Handshakes often are superficial acts. Giving or receiving a hug demonstrates understanding and care. When we risk embracing someone we are acknowledging a bond.

2.   Do a favor for a friend without being asked. Going that extra mile for people, anticipating their needs, also can bring us satisfaction. We all need help from time to time, and it may be reassuring for others to know that they can count on us.

3.   Let others help when they offer to do so. In the past we likely shunned the help that others offered. We worried that accepting help was a sign of weakness. Yet the truth is that we cannot function in this world alone. We need support. Letting others nourish and sustain us is the basis of genuine intimacy.

Adam and Eve Revisited

In the light of all we have been learning, another examination of the garden scene may be helpful.

The LORD God took the man and put him in the Garden of Eden to work it and take care of it.

And the LORD God commanded the man, "You are free to eat from any tree in the garden; but you must not eat from the tree of the knowledge of good and evil, for when you eat of it you will surely die."

The LORD God said, "It is not good for the man to be alone. I will make a helper suitable for him."

Now the LORD God had formed out of the ground all the beasts of the field and all the birds of the air. He brought them to the man to see what he would name them; and whatever the man called each living creature, that was its name. (Genesis 2:15-19)

Prior to their sin, Adam and Eve communed with God unhindered. Theirs was an uncomplicated and natural relationship. Adam and Eve felt completely safe with God, free and open.

The fact that Adam and Eve were naked demonstrates their openness—physically, emotionally, spiritually, and mentally. God's plan for humanity is based on this standard of a pure, natural relationship. Shame and deception run counter to God's plan.

Adam and Eve's initial relationship with God points to four truths about fellowship with our Creator.

1. **God wants to know us.** Genesis 3:8 says, "Then the man and his wife heard the sound of the LORD God as he was walking in the garden in the cool of the day." Adam and Eve communicated daily with God. He actually came to the garden to meet with them. Since God no longer physically walks among us, our prayers become our lifeline to him.

    In the past, praying might have been difficult for us. Feeling imperfect, we may have feared being judged or found out. But now, through grace, we can view God in a new way. Prayer can be like talking with a close friend. Our prayers can be simple or formal, whatever feels right for us. We have nothing to fear. God is a powerful God, yet his desire is not for power. It is for love, gentleness, meekness, and kindness. Seeing that God understands us and genuinely wants to listen to our needs makes us wish to share our true self.

2. **God believes in us.** Adam and Eve were given great responsibilities. They were in complete charge of the Garden of Eden. God even asked Adam to name all of the animals. Though God did not base his love on Adam and Eve's abilities, he certainly affirmed their capabilities. In the same way, God believes in our talents and skills. Knowing this gives us the courage to take risks and to feel closer to him.

3. **God loves us unconditionally.** God was not a hard taskmaster; Adam and Eve had only one rule to keep. There were no rules about stealing, swearing, or other areas of conduct. These were not needed because the love between Adam and Eve and God was solid and did not depend on performance.

    Rules are required when relationships break down. This is what happened to Adam and Eve after the fall. However, God sent Christ to repair humanity's broken relationship. Through Christ's actions, God's unconditional love awaits us. All we need to do is accept it.

4. **God understands us and empathizes with us.** Seeing that it was not good for Adam to be alone, God created Eve. God will not abandon us. He knows our needs. We can always count on him. Jesus said,

So do not worry, saying, "What shall we eat?" or, "What shall we drink?" or, "What shall we wear?"

For the pagans run after all these things, and your heavenly Father knows that you need them.

But seek first his kingdom, and his righteousness, and all these things will be given to you as well. (Matthew 6:31-33)

Shame has alienated us from God by distorting our image of him. In the process of becoming free from shame, our concept of God will naturally change. We will begin to realize that God wants to know us, he understands and empathizes with us, he believes in us, and he loves us unconditionally. Reminding ourselves of these truths draws us back to our loving Father, ending our alienation.

Summary

As we have changed our identities, we no longer may be willing to settle for superficial relationships. We need to confront current shaming relationships, challenging them to become more authentic and loving. We also may need specific skills to counteract shame, regardless of the source. Left unchecked, shame will erode our self-worth and interrupt our process of grace-full renewal.

We probably also will want to develop new relationships to support the important work we have done. First, however, we must be our own friend. And honesty, forgiveness, respect, and nurturance remain fundamental to our new truthful lifestyle.

The Genesis account of Adam and Eve's original relationship with God indicates that theirs was a natural, unfettered union.

God's plan for us was and is exciting. He promises us that he wants to know us, he believes in us, he understands and empathizes with us, and he loves us unconditionally.

How glorious it is to know that shame was not part of our Creator's intent for us. With great joy we can celebrate the new life God wants for us!

EPILOGUE

As the oldest child in my family and a pastor's son, I felt pressured to live up to extremely high standards. My father was very disciplined. He read the Bible daily and rarely showed any deep emotions. As I observed my father over the years I came to believe that I needed to emulate his lifestyle or I would fall out of God's favor. I assumed that I needed to be unemotional, just as my father was, and I feared doing anything that would bring harm on his ministry. These early experiences contributed to my Adam and Eve Complex.

As I look back on my life, my first Adam and Eve belief was that I was "unacceptable" if I got angry, broke any rules of the church (of which there were many), or somehow disappointed my parents.

My second belief was that I could not "count on" others. My father never seemed to need anyone, so I mistakenly thought I shouldn't, either.

The third belief was that I had "no choice" but to live by my father's rules, so I had no way to make my life better. This last belief contributed greatly to my feelings of depression.

Admitting that I had problems and dealing with them was a long, painful process. My first steps came in college. A professor asked me to join a group he was leading that dealt with self-awareness. I was terrified, yet I wanted to understand my anguish. I don't think I said a word for the first several months the group met. However, after a time I discovered that I wasn't alone. Other Christians like me had problems, too.

I was surprised that I could be accepted even after admitting my shortcomings. I didn't have to be my father to be in God's graces, and I didn't have to be as perfect as Jesus Christ to be a good Christian.

Since that time I have been able to share with my father my pain over trying to play the role of the perfect pastor's child, and he has shown some acceptance and understanding. Even more important, I have grieved this and other disappointments of my childhood and learned to let go of that constricting role I had established for myself.

I also have had to work through my own anger with God, whom I had envisioned as an unreasonable taskmaster instead of a nurturing and loving God. This symbolic change happened over many years, but one significant breakthrough came while I was attending a spiritual retreat.

Late one night, after a session that focused on grace, I had a dream that I was flying. I believe my ability to fly was a sign that I needed to be myself, to break free from my old ways of thinking, acting, and living—my Adam and Eve Complex. This dream revealed to me that God would love me regardless of whether or not I lived up to all of the "right" Christian standards.

When I discovered that God could accept me in all my imperfection I was able to let grace into my life and move much closer in my relationship with God, self, and others.

I am not saying that now all of my relationships are wonderful or perfect. I am still very much "in process." But shame no longer has the power over me it once did. I know now that I don't have to be perfect in order to be loved, and I am passing on this word of hope to you.

Continue to seek the truth—in your life and in God. Don't be afraid to look inside yourself. Trust me—you will find something beautiful at your core. God does accept you, and others will, too. Through the power of grace and love, shame dies in defeat.

The Tenets of Shame

Tenet One: Faulty Beliefs

Faulty belief number one:
I am worthless and unacceptable to God, myself, and others.

Faulty belief number two:
Others will abandon me. I therefore must meet my own needs.

Faulty belief number three:
Life will never get better, and I am helpless to change it.

Tenet Two: Protective Actions

Hiding from God, others, and self.

Tenet Three: Deceptive Lifestyle

A lifestyle based on self-deception, lies, and anger which leave the individual alienated and estranged from God, self, and others.

Grace-full Renewal

New Grace-driven Beliefs

1. God has given me value and worth. I am acceptable.

2. God has not abandoned me. With Christ I can learn to trust others to meet my needs.

3. Grace empowers me to change my life for the better.

Genuine Actions

I can be truly open and genuine with God, self, and others.

Truthful Lifestyle

A lifestyle based on honesty, respect, forgiveness, and nurturance that brings me into communion with God, self, and others.